Crossroads

Dennis Rogers

The News and Observer

Raleigh, N.C.

Also by Dennis Rogers:
Home Grown
Second Harvest

Library of Congress Catalog Number 84-61699

ISBN 0-935400-10-9 (Hardcover)
ISBN 0-935400-11-7 (Softcover)

Cover photograph by John Rottet

Artwork by Jackie Pittman
Cover design by Dot Stell

The first one was for Mama, the second one was for my daughters and this one is for my family: for Thom, Pris, Bob and Dale for teaching an only child what it is like to have brothers and sisters; for Nancy for passing through my life; for the bikers and the cowboy pickers and Buzz and Tommy in Greenville for their brotherhood and Saturday nights; for gentle Guy for being my friend and literary midwife and never being too busy to care and encourage; and especially for Gail, for everything.

Contents

A Few Words About Bubba

Bubba was in no mood to be trifled with.

Doreen, the head barmaid at the Way Out Yonder Saloon, had picked up his beer can while he was standing at the juke box. She said she thought it was empty. Bubba thought that was a pretty flimsy excuse since there was at least an inch left in it. He figured she was trying to get him to buy another one so she could get another tip.

"What's wrong with you, Doreen?" he yelled when he got back to the bar. He wasn't really mad but he had to yell to be heard over Kris Kristofferson singing "He's a walking contradiction, partly truth and partly fiction." Bubba liked that song. He thought it was about him.

"I'm real sorry, Bubba," Doreen said, "I don't know where my mind is today."

Bubba figured she was heartbroken over what had happened the night before. Her boyfriend Scooter had last been seen riding off with some blonde honey named Peaches perched on the back of his Harley.

"What's wrong?" said Bubba, trying to be kind and not too nosy.

"It's this book I've been reading," Doreen said. "I picked this thing up and I can't put it down. It's by that feller who works down at The News and Observer. You know him, he comes in here a lot. Name's Dennis Rogers."

"Know him? Hey, he's the one who made me famous when he wrote about me and my brother Yuppie," Bubba said. "He's all right. Say he's got a new book out? Let me see that thing."

Bubba picked up the book and looked at it. There he was on the cover, that Rogers feller he'd taken two dollars off playing eight ball.

"What's it about?" Bubba asked Doreen. "It's about 200 pages," Doreen said and then broke up laughing at her own cheap joke. Bubba did not laugh. Bubba did not get the joke.

"Really, it is a collection of about a hundred of his favorite columns," she said. "Most of them were written in the last three years, stuff he wrote after his second book called 'Second Harvest.' This one is called 'Crossroads.'"

"Am I in it?" Bubba asked. He had never been in a book before and the idea made him happy. It made him so happy he gave Doreen a fifteen cent tip, something he hardly ever did before 11 p.m.

"Yeah, Bubba, you're here," Doreen said. "You and a lot of those good folks from Down East. He's got some funny stuff in here and some stuff about things that bug him, like the monster who lives in his basement and some stories about his kids and there's a few two-hanky tearjerkers that made my mascara run.

"He's even got the column in here that made people so mad they tried to get him fired."

Bubba took the book and wandered over to a table. He sat down and started reading. He was reading away when a commotion broke out at the front door. He looked up and saw it was Scooter, Peaches and Doreen. They were having a discussion about the sawed-off pool cue Doreen was waving at Peaches. Scooter was trying to hide behind the juke box.

"I'll thank y'all to hold it down to a dull roar," he yelled. "I'm reading about me and my friends and the places we go and the things we do and the things we think and talk about.

"I hate a bunch of illiterates."

The discussion stopped. They had never heard Bubba use such language. They wandered over and started reading over his shoulder. Scooter slid his arm around Doreen and gave her roll a little pinch. She giggled and snuggled a little closer.

Peaches saw what was happening and decided it was Bubba she really liked anyway. She started tickling his ear lobe with her pinky. They were all so happy.

Bubba turned the page.

Why don't you do the same thing?

Well, If You Ask Me . . .

You may have heard of Yuppies by now.

That's what they call the Young Urban Professionals who eat green spaghetti, hang out in bars that have a lot of ferns, drive BMW's to health spas and will spend enough money this year on jogging suits to buy a good set of recaps for a pickup.

I am not a Yuppie.

I am a Bubba.

Bubba: Boys Unburdened by Briefcases, BMW's and Aerobics.

If you are a Yuppie, you know it, and so do those around you. But perhaps you are really a Bubba at heart.

Things Bubbas like to drink: sweet iced tea so dark you can't see through it, anything cold in a longneck bottle, Wild Turkey and 7Up, milk with Mama's biscuits, and whatever is put in front of you when some happy drunk buys a round for the house.

Words Bubbas would never use: Ciao, upscale, condo, user-friendly, Cuisinart and mega-bucks.

Vehicles Bubbas like to drive: 1966 GTO's, all pickup trucks, Harley-Davidson motorcycles and vans of more than one color as long as one of them is primer red.

Some Bubba definitions: Briefcase: a case of Coors with two bottles missing. Aerobics: driving 55 with both windows down in the pickup. Squash racket: selling homegrown squash in a roadside stand at inflated prices to Yuppies who think they're getting a bargain. Olive oil: Popeye's ugly girlfriend.

Bubba role models: Burt Reynolds (not in that wimpy "Starting Over" that Yuppies dearly love but in a good movie like "Smokey and the Bandit"), all stock car drivers except Darrell Waltrip, former Oakland Raiders coach John Madden and the U.S. Marine Corps or the 82nd Airborne Division.

Things Bubbas do not like to do on Saturday mornings: go to flea markets to look for precious porcelain figurines; take the paint off wicker furniture (shoot, Bubbas don't even like to sit on wicker furniture); water house plants, dust venetian blinds (particularly those little bitty ones); shave; or hang out in any store that sells dirt in plastic bags to men who drive station wagons.

What Bubbas do like to do on Saturday mornings: sleep, buy anything made of chrome, eat hot dogs for breakfast, go buy some beer for the afternoon basketball game, and wash cars, trucks, motorcycles.

Favorite Bubba music: Hank Williams, Jr., Willie Nelson when he used to sing country music, Lynyrd Skynyrd, Waylon Jennings, Kenny Rogers and Dolly Parton the first 200 times they sang "Islands In the Stream" on the radio, and always George Jones.

People Bubbas would like to hit in the mouth: Phil Donahue, Alan Alda, people who put bows in a dog's hair even if it is a poodle and deserves it, Al McGuire, people who sell cemetery plots by telephone, Boy George and Michael Jackson.

Things Bubbas will not eat no matter how hungry they are: pate (which is a fancy name for liver pudding, which is good), raw vegetables that some people try to pawn off as munchies at parties instead of honest potato chips, anything that looks like it has already been eaten once, which includes most things from a food processor, tofu and raw fish.

Bubba heroes: the person who invented the sleeveless down jacket, the person who invented the in-dash cassette deck, the person who is bringing Lone Star beer to North Carolina, and Jacques Heim. What do you mean "Who is Jacques Heim?" He's the fellow who invented the bikini.

Some things you have to have to reach a perfect state of Bubba-hood, although that probably is unattainable: a wallet fastened to a wide black belt by a shiny chain; a wife or girlfriend (or both) who has two first names, neither of which is Buffy or Muffin; a custom pool cue in an imitation leather case that you know how to use; a four-wheel-drive pickup with lights on the roof and a dog to ride in the back; a belt buckle the size of a saucer; a friend who is a mechanic; and a payday every Friday.

The Bubba Ten Commandments: Thou shalt allow no sucker to talk about thy mother. Thou shalt take unto thee no jeans with designer labels. Thou shalt honor the name of Buck Knife and keep it sharp. Thou shalt never eat brunch on Sunday. Thou shalt not kill anything thou ain't planning to eat, with the possible exception of thy egg-sucking dog.

Thou shalt not wink at the girlfriend of anybody who has tattoos on his lips. Thou shalt not spit out the window of thy pickup when thou art being followed by a large number of motorcycles. Thou shalt not kick another man's dog unless it is becoming romantic with thy leg. Thou shalt not drive a Volvo unless thou art in Sweden, otherwise thou shalt walk first. Thou shalt never put Roman numerals after thy youngun's name.

Naps for Fretful Adults

The wisest boss I ever had was an Army captain.

We were a small group, 25 men assigned to the 191st Military Intelligence Detachment in the small village of Paju-ri, South Korea.

We were isolated from normal military units, so we could live pretty much as we pleased as long as we got the work done.

One of the things we did, on orders from our captain, was to take afternoon naps.

Lunch was 90 minutes long. We were to finish eating within 30 minutes and then sack out for one hour before going back to work.

The result was that the afternoon droop that infects most offices never hit ours. Some of us might be a little grumpy for the first 30 minutes after waking up but we did more work and worked later with more efficiency and less griping than any place I've worked before or since.

Look around your work place some day about 2:30 or 3 p.m. There is a sluggishness afoot that wasn't there in the morning. I suspect more paper clips get mangled and more doodles get doodled in midafternoon than at any other time. Daydreaming is rampant.

Time and people drag along. Lunch is resting heavily, minds are in neutral. People yawn and feel stupid.

Wouldn't a nap feel good?

I am convinced that if everyone took a nap once a day the world would be a better, more productive place to live.

A good nap recharges the batteries, it erases the petty grumps that make people testy and hard to get along with. It allows you to start all over. It works wonders, no matter when you do it.

Many people come home from work late in the afternoon in foul shape. The problems of work are compounded by the problems of home and the result is a decided flagging of the human spirit.

Arguments break out, people snap at each other, the evening is ruined and people go to bed mad at each other.

Try this: Come in from work, nod politely at everyone and announce that for the next hour you are not to be disturbed. Then go lie down and sleep for one hour. It may take awhile but after a few days of seeing your smiling, rested face an hour later the people around you will be grateful for your good cheer.

Sunday afternoons are probably the best nap times of all. Most people don't care much for Sunday afternoons. The Monday Morning Blues begin to intrude early in the day for many. A nap is just the ticket. I recommend two hours on Sunday, say 4:30 p.m. to 6:30 p.m. Then you get up feeling restored, eat supper and watch "60 Minutes."

Fretful children are sent to their rooms to take naps. Maybe it is time we did the same thing to fretful adults.

It takes practice to be a good napper. The biggest mistake that novice nappers make is to overdo it. Taking off all your clothes and getting under covers is not napping. That is going to sleep.

A proper nap is taken on top of the covers, with perhaps a light blanket on chilly days. You should keep your clothes on. They remind your body that this is a nap, not a major zonk-out.

Training yourself to wake up on time also takes practice. It is best to have someone standing by in case your mental alarm clock fails, but you'll be surprised how good you'll get after awhile. Experienced nappers can time it within five minutes.

A short nap also can save your life. I travel a lot and when I get sleepy on a long haul I'll pull over, lock the doors and lean back. Twenty minutes spent lightly napping makes the rest of the trip go a lot faster and safer.

Grab naps where you can. Go out to your car at lunch and

crash. Televised golf is the best nap inducer in the world, but an old book you've read before works pretty good. Tell everyone that you don't get home from work until an hour and a half after you really do, and use the peace and quiet to nap before the phone starts ringing.

The anti-nappers won't understand, of course, because they are the go-go people for whom napping is a waste of valuable time. Let them criticize all they want as long as they do it quietly.

Miscellaneous Musings on Life

Random thoughts on an autumn day too pretty to spend getting seriously involved in work:

Only people with enough money to buy everything say, "Money isn't everything." It might not be everything, but they sure hang on to it as if it were.

When you open those jackpot game cards they give you at supermarkets and burger joints, do you really expect to win something? Of course you do. We remain a people with strike-it-rich dreams.

Children are the first to laugh when Mama and Daddy play and the first to cry when they fight.

The truest symbol of authority is a clipboard.

Talking to someone who is wearing mirrored sunglasses is not that much fun.

Does anyone besides me remember singer Bobby Sherman?

Every year, fashion experts predict that the miniskirt is coming back, but it never does.

Has there ever been a school class that did make the world a better place to live, as they were challenged to do at their high school graduation?

Who buys those ugly clothes you see in the stores? That question is posed by the only person alive who will admit that he once bought a silver lame Mao jacket. But I only wore it once.

Why does actor Rip Torn call himself that? His real name, by the way, is Elmore Torn.

Why do the best late shows come on TV the night before the morning you have to get up early?

Pregnant women do have a special glow. It comes from an increase in oil in their skin and hair.

The prettiest line that Shakespeare wrote is, "Good night sweet prince and flights of angels sing thee to thy rest." It is from Hamlet.

If it is funny when black comics like Richard Pryor make fun of white people, why isn't it funny when white comics make fun of blacks? Maybe we still have a long way to go.

Seeing your name on a tombstone in a strange cemetery makes you wonder what the person who shared your name was like.

The best feeling things in the world are new socks and clean sheets.

Everyone knows clean cars drive better than dirty ones.

Doesn't it make you feel good when a former teacher remembers your name? And isn't it awful when they don't?

The best morning is a sunny Saturday morning; the worst night is a rainy Sunday night.

Don't you love it when you look into another car and see somebody singing along with the radio? I always try to find the station they're listening to.

Nothing will turn a man into a blubbering fool quicker than trying to explain to a clerk in a hardware store the exact thingamajig he needs to fix his whatzits.

A boy meeting his new girlfriend's parents is not half as tense as the father he's meeting. The father is thinking exactly what the boy thinks he's thinking.

You probably know more people you would rather not be stuck in an elevator with than people you'd like to have around at a time like that.

There are more ugly babies than ugly puppies.

Sometimes you can tell by the way a telephone rings that no one is going to answer it.

Your car won't do it when you're standing there telling the mechanic what it has been doing.

The hardest salesman to say a flat "no" to is an insurance salesman. Guilt is the best sales tool of all.

Good losers are easier to find than good winners.

It is a wise parent who never tells embarrassing stories about their children at a family reunion, especially when the children are standing there squirming.

Nag About Horse Meat Hoagies

Immigrants of the Northern persuasion have, from time to time, accused me of saying unkind things about them in this space.

It is an unfair accusation, of course. All I have done is gently point out the error of their ways.

I have done my best to make them feel at home in our fair land. I have coached them in how to speak the Mother Tongue and to eat grits without shuddering.

I have done my best to introduce their tattered palates to the native delicacies, to wit, how to pour peanuts into a Pepsi and where to find the Sacred Grub that is barbecue.

I have urged them to take unto themselves a wife with two first names or a husband with two last names.

And what do I get for my trouble? Am I praised as a goodly person who saw a need and tried to answer it? I should be treated like Squanto, the Indian who taught the original Pilgrims how to plant corn and not to starve to death.

But no, Yankees and Yankee sympathizers alike accuse me of being prejudiced, close-minded and chauvinistic.

I may be all that. Southerners may be, as portrayed on television by Yankee producers, directors and actors, ignorant hillbillies who race around back roads and talk real dumb.

But by cracky, we don't eat horse meat.

They do up North, you know.

I hope you didn't miss the story. It was wonderful.

The New York City Health Department (a Yankee front group) issued a permit allowing a Yankee company to sell horse meat on the streets in New York City.

I believe in free enterprise as much as the next fellow, and the company, Chevalean Foods of Hartford, Conn., has every right to invest its money and see what happens.

What did happen?

Did New Yorkers react with horror at the idea of munching the relatives of such legendary horses as Trigger, Man-O-War, Fury and Mister Ed?

Did New Yorkers storm the pushcarts and heap physical and verbal abuse on the vendors as they so richly deserved?

Are you kidding?

They not only bought horse burgers (85 cents with cheese) and horse steak sandwiches, They lined up in the rain for the honor.

I am suitably appalled.

Even the U.S. military services, which will cook anything and call it chow, do not serve horse meat.

Ah, you say, this boy is a provincial fool. Does he not know that in France horse meat is a delicacy? Yeah, I know that. I also know that the French are a foolish people. My proof? The French invented the metric system. So much for the horse-eating French.

And vegetarians in our midst might say, hey, what's the difference? Horse meat, beef, fish? Well, they're just wrong. They won't even eat a barbecue sandwich piled high with slaw and wash it down with a Pepsi, so what kind of credibility do they have?

Cows were born to be eaten. They are too dumb for anything else. I have yet to see a bovine with a lick of sense. Ditto for hogs, chickens and, the dumbest of all God's creatures, the turkey.

What it all comes down to is that truly civilized people eat only ugly and/or dumb animals. I do not eat venison. I saw the movie "Bambi," thank you, and, while exceedingly dumb, deer are undeniably cute. I also do not eat rabbits and raccoons for the same reason.

Eat a horse? Never. I grew up in movie theaters and I saw too many noble steeds save their masters too many Saturday afternoons to have one of their friends or relatives over for dinner. Had it not been for Trigger, Roy Rogers (King of the Wild West Wimps) would have been done for any number of times.

But you can't tell Yankees and Yankee sympathizers that. No sir, they're up there standing in the rain waiting for a chance at horse burgers.

Just think of it. Black Beauty grows old and becomes brunch for a Yankee subway mugger. Secretariat is slowed and is up to the fetlocks in a quiche (another highly suspect Yankee/French invention).

One last thing. I know as surely as the Dixie dew covers the kudzu that some smarty-pants Yankee or Yankee sympathizer is going to say, "Hey youse guys, hows about dem chitterlings? I wouldn't eat nunna dat stuff."

Nod and admit that, yes, we eat chitlins' and then tell him about the casings on that good link sausage he had for breakfast.

Trigger-burgers, indeed.

In Defense of That Holy Grub

People are always saying to me, "Dennis, tell us what is wrong with the world."

Since you asked, I'll tell you.

What is wrong with the world is that barbecue, that succulent provider of nourishment, that Holy Grub which is always what you want to eat when you don't know what you want to eat, that heavenly blending of delicate flavors, that faithful friend, has been maligned, libeled, trod upon and lied about.

What has me, perhaps the mildest person you know, in such a swivet are the following words, published in the Arizona Republic, explaining to our Western neighbors the definition of North Carolina barbecue:

"The meat is very much a stewed kind of thing. It is very well-cooked, chopped and then cooked until it is very stringy and falling apart. The sauce is in with it, not added later. It is not quite as tomatoey as the Texas style. It definitely has a lot of cayenne in it.

"I suspect pork is at least as popular if not more popular than beef. Then they do a combination, mixed together."

And here is how, fellow barbecue eaters, we are supposed to cook our North Carolina barbecue. You mix up garlic salt, oregano, salad oil, vinegar, fresh tomatoes, tomato sauce and a whole bunch of cooked and shredded pork and stew it in a crockpot all day.

Lord have mercy, what are they doing in the name of the barbecue?

I feel the vapors coming on. I think I'd better lie down for a spell.

"This barbecue is best refrigerated overnight for use the next day," writes the author of this outrage.

This barbecue is best thrown in the swamp because a hog wouldn't eat it.

Now, I don't know much. I don't know how to divide fractions, I don't know why there is no blue food, and I don't know how to keep score in tennis, but I do know that mess is not barbecue.

Stewed meat in a crockpot?

Whatever happened to a fresh, 90-pound pig over a wood or charcoal fire in a portable cooker hooked to the back of a gun-rack-equipped pickup truck.

How about those old boys with a Miller in one hand, smoke curling in their eyes, gnawing on a test rib and allowing as how it may need a few more minutes because it's been on the fire only nine hours?

Where does the author talk about the cookers taking breaks by pitching horseshoes, telling lies and discussing the relative merits of Darrell Waltrip vs. either of those Allison boys? Of course, Richard Petty is still the king.

I didn't read any mention of dogs chasing boys and vice versa throughout the cooking grounds, both species learning right off that you don't get to close to the fire or the men tending it but once.

I must have missed the part about the aunts gathered near a tree, sitting in straining aluminum lawn chairs with riotously colored strips of sturdy nylon holding them in place like a high-tech cargo net. Here there is talk of life, birth, marriage and death, of things close to home and of favorite afternoon stories.

Where is mention of the uncles, gathered over by a dusty pickup truck, learning and spitting and disturbed about the state of things in general? Nothing seems to be going as well, or at least the same, as it used to go.

I missed the strong young ones preening themselves in car windows when they think no one is looking, plotting just how to catch the eye of a passing fancy. The burning question is, did you see who she was with in the Hardee's parking lot last night, and didn't somebody tell me they had broken up?

Then, as if by some mystical sign, one of the cookers whose name is not Buddy (but that's what everybody calls him), announces that the pig is ready, and there is a genteel but determined movement, and you'd better step lively as a line forms to grab plates piled high with pig, steaming Brunswick stew and boiled potatoes, slaw, a big handful of hush puppies and a glass of iced tea so dark that you have to hold it toward the setting sun to see through it.

Everybody says the same thing, "Lordy, they gave me too

much; I'll never eat all this," but that's a story. They will eat every bite and might even have a little banana pudding, just to get the grease out of their mouths.

I didn't read that in the Arizona Republic while I was reading how you can cook barbecue in a crockpot while you go to spend the day in an air-conditioned office.

And did I miss the part about when the eating's done, how you put all the paper plates in a rusted 55-gallon oil drum standing on end and burn them, and how the little boys stick sticks in the fire until the end glows and make bright circles in the night with their red-orange pencils?

And where was the little girl who catches her first firefly and runs to her daddy and tells him to keep it for her while she goes off in search of another? And her daddy does, looking a little foolish and feeling good and hoping like crazy that the bug doesn't die before she gets back.

The young couples with little ones to put to bed leave first, and soon they all go, leaving the dying embers and the stories floating in the still air, borne on a haze of rich smoke and ripe meat.

Sorry Arizonans, but cooking barbecue isn't as easy as you might think.

The Strange Miseries of January

January is easily my least favorite month, and it takes forever to get over.

Anticipation of the holidays gets you through November and December, but January hangs on like a headache. The Christmas toys are broken, the new wool sweater you got for Christmas was washed in hot water and fits only a thin poodle with long legs. (Why don't the sleeves get shorter when they shrink?) And the bills have arrived.

I got a bill the other day. It was my heating bill. I opened it and laughed. You always read about some poor schnook getting a bill for some astronomical amount, and it turns out the computer went weird and added a bunch of zeroes to the bill. That's what I though had happened to me.

Wrong. I really owe my soul to the gas company. And all I could think about was that December wasn't all that cold, and I thought I had kept the thermostat set really low.

Cabin fever is what they call the January Blues. It does strange things to people. Witness what is happening in Kinston and New Bern.

Those two usually friendly towns, separated by only 31 miles of concrete and tobacco fields, have declared a joke war on each other.

In New Bern they say:

What do you call 16 potholders and a black velvet painting of Elvis? The Kinston Arts and Crafts Fair.

What is the difference between Kinston and a can of motor oil? The oil is refined.

Why don't they have artifical turf at Kinston High School? Because the homecoming queens wouldn't have a place to graze.

What do you call a handsome man in Kinston? A visitor.

What is the difference between a Kinston girl and a garbage can? The garbage can gets taken out once a week.

Honk if you're from New Bern. Get your mother to hang out the window and bark if you're from Kinston.

People from Kinston don't like bananas. There isn't much left to eat once you throw away the cob.

In Kinston they say:

Did you hear about the problem with the New Bern garbage service? They only deliver once a week.

Did you hear why New Bernians have bad skin? It isn't acne, it's scars from trying to learn to eat with a fork.

Did you hear why New Bern girls are so ugly? They bob for oysters.

There is no use asking New Bernians to act as human beings. They don't do impressions.

At a college reunion, everybody who had a degree was asked to stand and call it out. A lady from New Bern stood and said "102.4."

This battle has been raging for a couple of weeks in the pages of the New Bern Sun-Journal and the Kinston Daily Free Press. Both sides claim victory. As a neutral judge, I proclaim it a draw. The agony caused by both sides in this War of the Groaner is inhuman.

But that is what happens in January. People call February the presidents' month because Washington and Lincoln were born in that short little month.

January has a few more presidents' birthdays than February,

but look who they are: Millard Fillmore (Jan. 7), Richard Nixon (Jan. 9), William McKinley (Jan. 29) and Franklin D. Roosevelt (Jan. 30). And I'll bet you forgot to send a card.

Do not hand me that Mother Nature jive about January being the time of resting when the earth prepares for the coming spring. Balderdash. Mom Nature is as cold as I am and refuses to have anything to do with January.

Beautiful month you say? People who say that could find something nice about a runny nose.

I'm not the only crazy around this month. I received the following letter last week that claimed to be from Playgirl magazine, but I don't think it was:

"We wish to thank you for your letter and pictures. We will not, however, be able to use your body in our centerfold at this time.

"On a scale of one to 10, your body was rated a minus two. The rating was done by a panel of women 65 to 75 years old. We tried to have it rated by our panel of women 18 to 32 years old, but we could not get them to stop laughing long enough."

Just last week there was a story in the paper that said boxing was dangerous. After exhaustive research, it was learned that getting bashed repeatedly in the brain by very strong men is not good for you. Kenneth Buffkin hit me in the head in the fourth grade, and I could have told them it hurt.

Excuse me, but I've had all the strangeness I can handle. Call me when it's February.

Spontaneous Human Combustion

Mary Hardy Reeser was last seen sitting in a comfortable easy chair in her retirement home in St. Petersburg, Fla., July 1, 1951.

Her son, a doctor who lived nearby, had given the 67-year-old widow two sleeping pills. When he left her early that evening, she was wearing slippers and a rayon-acetate nightgown.

The next person to enter the room was a neighbor, Mrs. P.M. Carpenter. What Mrs. Carpenter found 12 hours later is a classic case of what has come over the centuries to be called Spontaneous Human Combustion.

Mrs. Carpenter smelled smoke early that next morning. When she tried to open the door to Mrs. Reeser's small apartment, the door knob was too hot to grasp.

Mrs. Carpenter called for help. When rescuers arrived and opened the door, a gust of hot air rushed out.

Mrs. Reeser's easy chair had been reduced to a few twisted springs. The apartment walls and ceiling were covered in a black, oily soot but only above the four-foot level.

There was no offensive smell and no fire damage to the rest of the apartment. A pile of dry newspapers inches from the chair did not catch fire. Yet, Mrs. Reeser had literally burned up.

Fire investigators had a simple answer. Mrs. Reeser dropped a cigarette onto her gown and burned to death.

Maybe. But that answer does not satisfy the large number of people, some serious scientists and some wide-eyed followers of the bizarre, who say it was Spontaneous Human Combustion.

They quote people like John Grenoble, a lecturer on cremation who says a corpse in a crematorium is burned at 2,200 degrees for 90 minutes and then 1,800 degrees for up to two hours and when it is all over, workers still have to pulverize the remains to duplicate Mrs. Reeser's condition.

What created a fire that hot in an unheated apartment? Why did such a blaze not burn down the entire building? Why were the newspapers left untouched inches away?

You run into questions like that when you research Spontanteous Human Combustion. It is an event reported regularly since 1673 with more than 300 cases documented.

There is a similarity to all of them. People, for reasons that no one knows, burst into flame and burn with an incredibly intense heat until they are consumed. Items nearby often are not even singed. Witnesses who have seen it happen report that the fire seemed to come from within the person, not from some external source. The handful who have survived report that an intense blue flame burst through their skin from inside.

Phyllis Newcombe, a 22-year-old British woman, burst into flame on a dance floor and burned to death in front of a terrified crowd of dancers in 1938.

Billy Thomas Peterson of Pontiac, Mich., while attempting to commit suicide by breathing carbon monoxide inside his car in 1957, ignited and burned to death. His clothes did not catch fire while a plastic religious statue on the car dashboard melted.

There are any number of explanations available, none of them satisfactory to me. Most scientists discount the notion that people burn from within. Most fire and police investigators say that it cannot and does not happen.

Some researchers say the victims were all drunkards and somehow the alcohol-saturated body caught fire, usually brought on by a crisis that released electrical energy within the brain. Others say the victims were all fat and the fat caught fire.

But I've done some checking. From what I've been able to find out, the victims have ranged from 11 months old to 114 years old, drinkers and abstainers, fat people and skinny people, an almost even number of men and women.

One researcher writing in Science Digest says there is possibly something called a "subatomic pyrotron" and that bodies are consumed by an internal chain reaction, a process similar to what goes on in a nuclear power plant.

What it comes down to is that no one knows. It may all be an hysterical fraud. But apparently hundreds of people have burned to death when there was no logical reason or way for them to do so.

Take Dr. J. Irving Bently, a 92-year-old Pennsylvania physician who burned to death standing in his aluminum walker. The fire reached an estimated temperature of 3,000 degrees. Dr. Bentley was amost completely consumed. Yet, the rubber tips on the legs of his walker did not melt.

By my definition, that is one baffling puzzle.

A Spot of Pity for the Nerds

It is time someone spoke up for the lowly nerd.

I can't think of anyone better qualified than me to do it. You see, I used to be a nerd.

Of late, we have been overrun with stories about preppies, jocks and freaks. Apparently those are the only three social classes allowed in public schools these days. Private schools only allow preppies.

Preppies dress rich. Labels are everything; looking alike is in. If you aren't in pink and green and khaki, you'd best not show your silly face. Preppies like to grow up to be — or marry —

lawyers. You can tell adult male preppies from pink-and-green juvenile ones by their blue blazers with gold buttons, gray slacks, blue shirts with button-down collars, black shoes and narrow maroon ties. Adult female preppies still look like juvenile preppies.

The jocks are the athletes. They are big enough to wear any color T-shirt they want with their low-slung jeans and name-brand sneakers.

The freaks are everyone else. It is a too-broad category encompassing rednecks, cowboys, jerks, exchange students and the occasional free thinker.

But what about the true nerds? They deserve better. They deserve their own category.

Without the nerds, who would everyone else be glad they weren't? Who would even the dumbest airhead have to look down on if not for the honorable nerd?

Nerds are the only people who don't care what other people think. Who else would wear misshapen garbardine pants 2 inches above their ugly shoes? Who else would wear baggy white short-sleeved shirts month in and month out? Who else would put those little plastic holders in their shirt pockets to keep a colorful array of ballpoint pens from leaking on those drippy shirts? Who else would get their hair "cut" instead of "styled"?

Only a true nerd would do those things — but not because he is brave and doesn't mind the taunts, and not because he thinks it looks good. It's because the nerd just never thinks about his appearance. A nerd thinks only about what is practical.

I know. I used to be a nerd. I used to think white cars were best because they were cheap and didn't show dirt. Now I am cool and pay more for paint and have to wash the thing a lot.

A nerd chooses clothes that cover his nakedness, don't cost much and drip dry. A nerd loves double knit and discount stores.

I know. I used to be a nerd. My clothes lasted forever and my budget was healthy. Now I am cool and my name is known in clothing stores that have carpets and I am very broke.

A nerd thinks a hat is something to either keep the sun off or the heat in. It is not a statement of style or a place for advertising.

I know. I used to be a nerd. Now I am cool: I spend $30 for a stylish cowboy hat that I would never wear within three miles of any kind of livestock.

A nerd thinks eyeglasses serve a purpose and, if the plastic frame breaks, tape holds it together very nicely.

I know. I used to be a nerd and could see just fine. Now I am cool and often I can't see much of anything.

A nerd listens to the radio because he knows you can hear any kind of music for free.

I know. I used to be a nerd. Now I am cool and no longer have an ordinary record player and radio. I have a "sound system." But I still listen to the radio because I cannot afford albums for my "sound system."

A nerd goes to the movies to be entertained. He leaves the movie with no unanswered questions.

I know. I used to be a nerd. Now I am cool and I go to "films." I don't know what a lot of them are about.

A nerd doesn't pretend to have all the answers.

I know. I used to be a nerd. Now I have all the answers. I just can't remember what the question was.

Footnotes to Human Comedy

I think we're being rude to kudzu.

Kudzu, the plant kingdom's equivalent of the possum, has been lambasted as a greedy plant that grows and grows and grows and covers everything in its path.

People make jokes about kudzu. Tale-tellers love the one about the bird dog on point that was covered in kudzu. I read a story from Charlotte a few years back about the fellow who bought a rundown house and after weeks of work discovered a full-sized swimming pool covered by kudzu. People laugh at kudzu.

I think such boorish behavior is just terrible.

It wasn't like kudzu begged to come to the South or sneaked in at night. It was perfectly happy living in Japan until some soil conservation types got desperate and bought it, like an agricultural slave. Alex Haley even ripped off the perfect name for a story about kudzu's origins: "Roots."

They wanted a plant that grew quickly, would stop erosion, was hardy enough to grow anywhere and would return nitrogen to the soil. Kudzu did all of that, in spades.

They used to have kudzu clubs, and plants were handed out like fans at a country funeral. Everyone loved kudzu at first. But love is fickle.

All kudzu did was what it was supposed to do. One day men looked at a kudzu patch and said, "Stop growing."

Being a Japanese plant, kudzu did not understand English, even Southern English, and it kept doing what it was supposed to do. It kept growing.

Now everyone hates it and tries to get rid of it and makes fun of it. Pretty inhospitable, I'd say.

Here is an all-purpose plant that works its little tendrils off for man and, just because it won't mind us, we get ugly.

Sure, the stuff will cover up anything that stands still, but tell the truth, isn't the stuff it covers up better covered up?

Kudzu does not eat pretty little cottages, in pleasant neighborhoods. Kudzu goes for rundown shacks that ought to be torn down anyway.

Kudzu does not eat natty little sports cars. Kudzu loves to munch on rusted out DeSotos.

OK, so it grows up the side of telephone poles. Do you have a warm spot in your heart for Ma Bell? Not me.

Kudzu does not cover up meadows where lambs gambol in the sunlight. Kudzu goes for those raw ravines where big snakes lurk. And since kudzu grows 4 feet deep in places, I'm not about to go in there and meet those serpents.

Thanks, kudzu.

And people say kudzu isn't good for anything. Ha, I scoff.

Wouldn't you love to plant a bunch of kudzu at each end of Hay Street in Fayetteville and watch it go to work?

Why don't we plant it around used car lots, the kind with the strings of lights and the orange pennants?

Anywhere in Durham would be nice, ditto Charlotte.

All it takes is imagination, the old "when life hands you a lemon, make lemonade" school of positive thinking.

If people insist on stripping kudzu from its adopted Southland, I have the perfect solution. With my idea, kudzu would be but a memory in 24 hours.

What you do is make it illegal. Pass a law that says smoking kudzu gets you stoned, like smoking marijuana. Make the law effective 24 hours after it is signed. Then stand back. The pot smokers, suddenly faced with an unlimited supply of weed, would descend on every kudzu patch from Tarboro to Tupelo.

Let the rumor out that, while the leaves will get you high, the roots will really get you ripped.

Dawn's early light would then reveal all the ugly stuff kudzu has covered all these years. We would have stacks of old tires where once we had interesting green humps. New rundown buildings would appear magically. Snakes would have no place to hide and probably would all move to my house.

Admire it, treat it like a guest in our country, make it feel welcome, put it to work, give its life meaning.

Just don't get in its way.

Why Not Tax Things That Bug People?

I always feel particularly civic-minded on that joyous day we get to pay income taxes.

It's the one day of the year when we get to show the Internal Revenue Service how much we love it by mailing in our free-will love offerings. Check or money order, please. Not even the government trusts the Postal Service with cash.

I refuse to acknowledge anyone who paid their taxes in January, and I absolutely will not discuss those sanctimonious people who get refunds from the IRS. They know no mercy, no compassion for those of us who haven't quite figured out how to get enough taken out of our paychecks to cover the tax and allow us to buy groceries at the same time.

What I would like to propose on Tax Day is a means to greatly lessen — if not eliminate — income taxes and at the same time greatly increase federal revenues while making America an infinitely better place to live.

What you do is tax those little things that bug people.

For instance, any woman seen in a discount store wearing her hair in curlers, would have to pay $5 for the privilege. If she wanted to take her screaming children with her, she would pay $5 a head — $7.50 if the little fellow rode in the cart and pulled merchandise off the shelf and drooled on it. And if that woman insisted on wearing coral-colored double-knit slacks that were too tight and too short, she would have to pay $10 for visual pollution. You wouldn't even have to have the rule in effect all week long. The government could pick up enough in Raleigh on Saturday afternoons to keep the Defense Department in bang-bang toys.

The people who make shoelaces would be taxed $100 for every tip that came off, requiring the owner to lick the nasty thing to make it go through the eyelet. And there would be a $200 fine for every shoelace that broke in the first six months; $250 if it broke on a Monday morning.

Any supermarket manager who has malfunctioning shopping carts would be taxed based on the malady: $5 for two carts permanently stuck together, $10 if the cart had a stuck wheel, and a hefty $25 if one wheel had a flat side that made it go "thump-thump-thump." All taxes would double if the supermarket also had a game going where you had to save little stamps, because they always cancel the game just when I'm getting close.

Furniture and bedding manufacturers who sew those "Do Not Remove Under Penalty of Law" tags on at the seams, so that when you do show your rebellious independence and remove the tag, the seam gives way and all the stuffing comes out, would be taxed $1,000 and then taken out and beaten up by a consumer posse.

Any product that advertises itself as "new and improved" or "extra-strength" or uses the words "maxi" or "mini" would have a mere $1 tax added because there are so many of them, and we don't want to appear greedy. What would we do with all the money?

Any North Carolina resident — who should know better — who claims that barbecue from any other part of the state is superior to the Eastern variety would have to pay $5 for each such heretical utterance.

Any sportscaster who says that football is a "game of inches" (yeah, 3,600 of the little things) will pay $500; any host of a television special who introduces a guest as a "close personal friend of mine" will pay $750; anyone who utters the word "superstar" or "legend" on the public airwaves will surrender his Visa card to the government and be forced to spend 12 hours in a small room with Al McGuire and Howard Cosell.

Politicians who announced that they were running for office would pay $10, but that would rise to $10,000 if they tried to be coy about it and pretended they weren't running when they really were.

Speaking of politicians, the only person allowed to refer to Secretary of State Thad Eure as "the oldest rat in the

Democratic barn" would be Eure himself. Any master of ceremonies at a political event who uttered those fateful words would be taxed $100.

Any company putting a commercial for hemorrhoid medicine on television would pay $1 million and be forced to warn viewers 60 seconds before they were shown.

These are only a few ideas to get the government started. There are others, like 50 cents for every broken cookie in the box, $10 for every mechanic who looks at your busted car and says, "Them kind will do that," and $100 for every doctor who makes you walk through the waiting room with a sample in your hand. But I'm going to save the rest until my government calls on me.

Are you listening, Ronnie?

Maybe Those Fences Need Mending

Neighbors can sure get unruly sometimes.

Next to your family, you have to put up with more aggravation from your neighbors than anyone you face in daily living.

And my neighbors are beginning to bug me.

Before my good neighbors John, Martha, Marilyn, Hugh and Faye get upset and let the air out of my motorcycle tires, let me hasten to point out that the neighbors I'm ticked off at are Virginia and South Carolina.

What is wrong with those people?

It has been accurately said that North Carolina is a valley of humility between two mountains of conceit. I say that North Carolina is a mountain of virtue surrounded by valleys of weirdness.

Let us first deal with our neighbors to the north, the high and mighty Virginians who think they are such hot stuff just because a bunch of presidents were born there.

Just who do they think they are?

First of all, they're trying to steal our water by pumping the border lakes dry so the people of Virginia Beach can take lots of showers.

But did they act like good neighbors and come over and say, "Hi there, can I borrow a cup of water?"

Of course not. They came up with this sneaky idea to run a pipeline from the border lakes to Virginia Beach and siphon those boys dry. That would be like your neighbor not asking you for a lift to the filling station for a can of gasoline but going out with a siphon hose and draining your pickup dry in the middle of the night.

It is an un-neighborly act, if you ask me.

And then, to show us how much they like having us as neighbors while they're drinking our water, they slap up a fence across the Outer Banks and tell us we can't drive into their precious state to take showers with the water they stole from us.

Let us turn our attention to South Carolina. I am willing to forgive them for claiming that Andrew Jackson was born in their state and for pulling out of the Atlantic Coast Conference. I don't care where they say Andrew Jackson was born (although it obviously was in North Carolina), and the University of South Carolina has suffered far more by pulling out of the ACC than we did when they left.

My problem with South Carolina is that it seems to be a state of oddballs, crooks and so-called barbecue with mustard on it.

Take Rep. John "Bubba" Snow, a South Carolina legislator from Georgetown.

Don't get me wrong; anyone named "Bubba" can't be all bad, but when he gets the nerve to have the shag proclaimed the official state dance of South Carolina and claims that it was invented in Columbia, you gotta wonder whether Ol' Bubba ain't a few bricks shy of a load.

Anyone with sand in their Weejuns knows full well the shag came from the beaches of North Carolina, specifically Atlantic and Carolina beaches. Certainly not from some dive called Fat Sam's in midstate South Carolina in the 1930s.

But what do you expect from a state that leads the South and most of the nation in crooked politicans?

According to U.S. Justice Department figures, 96 elected and appointed public officials in the Palmetto State were convicted of federal crimes between 1976 and 1982. Three of them were state senators.

By comparison, a whopping three North Carolina officials were nailed in the same period. Our politicians are a whole lot smarter or a whole lot more honest than theirs. I decline to guess which.

Only five other places in America had more convicted politicians than South Carolina. Two of them were New York City and Chicago.

A news item: On April 29 of this year, a Dragon anti-tank missile was found at one of the South Carolina welcome centers. What are these people doing, arming their border guards?

Another news item: In late April, a geographer ranked 277 areas of the country by how good they were as places to live.

Three of the top five places to live were in North Carolina. No. 1 (the Greensboro-High Point-Winston-Salem Triad), No. 2 (Asheville) and No. 4 (the Triangle).

Guess how many places in South Carolina made it to the top 25? The answer is none. All of South Carolina was beaten out by places like Pittsburgh. The quality of life obviously goes down the tubes when you put mustard sauce on a pig and call it barbecue.

Guess how many places in high-falutin' Virginia made it to the top 25? The answer is zip. Virginia was beaten out by three towns in West Virginia — Charleston, Wheeling and Huntington. See what happens when your basketball coach names his dog Dean Smith?

And just in case anyone thinks I'm being parochial, let me hasten to add I was born in Virginia and lived — albeit briefly — in South Carolina.

But I try not to talk about that, so keep it between you and me, huh? I wouldn't want it to get out.

TV Is Out to Get Southerners

Business people are appalled at the treatment they're getting from television these days.

They say they are portrayed as ruthless pirates of high finance, ready to sell their souls and the nearest poor widow down the creek for big bucks.

The poor dears.

Hey, Mr. Businessman, try being a Southerner if you want to know what it's really like to be sliced up by television.

With the shining exception of "The Andy Griffith Show," the only show about Southerners in which I could recognize a soul,

Southerners routinely are portrayed as fools of one kind or another. The only other groups so lambasted have to be New York cab drivers, bikers and Vietnam veterans.

It doesn't matter what kind of Southerner you are. Lord knows, the networks are not ageists or sexists when it comes to attacking Southerners. They make fun of us all.

Young Southern males often are cast in the image of the Duke boys, those bare-chested, tight-jeaned, petty criminals from television's all-time most insulting, mindless and boring show, the ever-popular "Dukes of Hazzard."

And they, God help us all, are the good guys, the heroes, the role models, the nice Southern boys.

They drive like speed freaks — never mind there may be a school bus around the next dusty curve — in cars with hot engines, jacked-up rear ends and no door handles.

And they yell "Yee-haw" a lot while they're careening across the county.

The non-heroic young Southern male is a beer-drinking, truck-driving, shifty-eyed tough who beats his women and kicks his dogs. He carries a knife, so watch out for him. He also is pretty slow when it comes to figuring out stuff.

Your average non-Southerner can outfox this ole boy in the wink of an eye.

Then there is the other end of the scale, the elderly Southern woman. Granny comes to mind from "The Beverly Hillbillies," the second-most insulting, mindless and boring show in video history.

She smoked a pipe and wore combat boots. She was a bootlegger and feisty as all get out. She also was ugly as last week's meat loaf. A lot like your grandmother, huh?

If business people think they're getting a raw deal on television, try being a Southern businessman. They are all fat, wear white suits, smoke cigars and have dark secrets hidden in their mansions. Each one has a vacuous blond girlfriend whose bust size exceeds her IQ by a spectacular margin. The girlfriends also have a taste for chewing gum and fancy drinks with umbrellas.

Old Southern men. Television really loves them. They are flinty-eyed old codgers who'd as soon shoot you as give you the time of day. A smooth-talking Yankee who gets lost on a back road and asks one of these geezers for directions gets a stare filled with ominous silence or some wornout routine about how you can't get there from here, young whippersnapper. The old boys say things like "young whippersnapper" a lot.

Southern preachers? Oh yes, television loves our men of the cloth. With their white suits and pastel ties and blow-dried hair, they are out-and-out thieves who offer eternal salvation for a check in the mail. They share their taste in girlfriends with the businessmen and just love stretch limousines.

The alternative to the slick Southern electronic preacher is the mean-eyed fanatic who looks like a demented Abraham Lincoln as he raves about fire and damnation. He wears black suits and always is skinny. His wife plays the piano.

Southern politicians are another fun bunch on television. Again, the white suits. But these suits are dirty and wrinkled, and the collars are rolled down over fat, sweaty necks. They favor well-chewed cigars and homilies and can be bought for the price of a big jug of stumphole whisky. They are dumb.

Middle-age Southern farmers, perhaps America's most harmless of creatures, come off like the locals in "Deliverance." They are dangerous people, gun-toters and perverts with bad skin, greasy hair and without the normal contingent of teeth.

But television most seems to love our Southern women. Wow, what dishes they are. Fresh from the Daisy Mae School of How to Dress Like a Trollop, they sashay around in cutoff jeans that reveal their assets to the world or wear those off-the-shoulder numbers that defy the laws of physics. They are dumber than a sack of turnips.

There is another kind of Southern woman you see in "serious works of art." She is a homely creature with stringy hair, a shapeless dress and a dirty youngun on her hip. Her old man has run off and left her with a passel of hungry mouths to feed and was last heard of over in Jefferson County, where he's done took up with some white trash.

Of course, let us not forget the Southern law enforcement officer. He favors mirror sunglasses, a potbelly and a well-used nightstick and says things like, "Boy, you done messed up in my county."

Southern aunts are fun. They are universally ding-a-lings, sensitive creatures with flowered dresses and great food who mourn mysterious lost loves.

It is always hot in the South you see on television, a kind of steamy, oppressive heat that makes people mean. Or sometimes it just makes them randy. Folks wipe sweat a lot. They never have air conditioning.

And let us not forget the Southern journalists. We wear suspenders a lot and favor funeral parlor fans while we rear back in our big chairs and cover up the skulldugery going on in our little burgs.

I have but one question. Where does Hollyweird get all those white suits?

Have the Heels Turned Red?

This smarmy feeling of brotherhood between fans of the University of North Carolina and N.C. State University is getting a little sickening, don't you think?

Tar Heels and Wolfpackers long have had one of the better blood rivalries in collegiate sports, and this togetherness since the Pack won the national championship is ruining a good thing.

OK, I'll confess, when State won I gave forth a moderate "whoopee" and — I shudder at the memory — a not-too-loud "How 'bout that Pack?"

I felt guilty the next day, of course, although I realized I was showing typical Tar Heel class in pulling for a fellow North Carolina team.

But that's the curse of being a Tar Heel. We're just too nice. We can't help it. Drink once from the Old Well and you're a better person for it.

We are destroying one of this state's oldest and finest traditions with this lovey-dovey mess. Whatever happened to those glory days of bumper stickers that read, "Teach a young child to hate State?" Give a quiet cheer for the Cardiac Pack if you must, but for goodness' sake, keep it to yourself.

The fault for this turn of events rests squarely on the shoulders of Jimmy Valvano. The man is simply too pleasant.

It was easy to hate State when Norm Sloan was there, but Jimmy makes it tough. He seems like such a nice guy, despite his job, and more Tar Heels than I like to admit are saying how much they enjoyed the NCAA tournament and Jimmy's antics.

Let's remember a couple of things, folks.

This Pack team beat Carolina in their regular season meeting and again in the second round of the ACC tournament. I'm going to cheer for someone who denied my beloved Tar Heels the ACC crown?

Yeah, you bet. And pigs fly.

That's why I thought it would be terrific if Jimmy V. took that job with the New Jersey Nets.

The man is dangerous to the feud and should have moved.

I don't want a lovable coach at State. I want someone like Lefty Driesell of Maryland. Now there's a man you can boo with all your Carolina Blue heart. What makes Lefty so much fun is that he would rather cuss his mama than lose to Carolina. He is Dean Smith's designated foil. He is perfect for the job.

Give me a guy like Terry Holland. I really can get on Terry, even if he is from Clinton, and it makes watching a Carolina-Virginia game a more intense pleasure. Holland and the Cavaliers are the only things on which State and Carolina fans are allowed to agree.

And that is how it should be.

Wasn't the Carolina-State rivalry more fun when Stormin' Norman was at State? Didn't you love to hate those plaid jackets and Mrs. Stormin' singing the national anthem? Wasn't it terrific when the Heels won and Norm wouldn't shake Dean's hand?

State fans, to their credit, have not let this championship fever temper their hatred for Carolina. The first things I saw were bumper stickers that read, "Wake, Carolina, Virginia — Breakfast of Champions."

And that didn't seem to make Tar Heels mad. We are taking this Carolina "ladies and gentlemen" thing too far.

I am sorely disappointed in Carolina fans in all this. Remember Heels, most State fans pulled for the Russians when we last played them.

I have a good friend, a fine woman who has pulled for the Heels when she didn't have to. She is a University of South Carolina graduate who lives among us and has shown the good sense to become a Tar Heel fan. She is not born and bred, but she has been faithful.

And what happened? This wonderful Tar Heel has adopted a cute, homeless kitten that she has named "Cozell" in honor of Mr. McQueen of the Wolfpack.

The sad part is that she likes the cat, unlike Terry Holland, who named his dog Dean Smith so he could kick him.

We must end this phony truce and get back to the dedication required to maintain an intense rivalry.

Tar Heels, ask yourself this: Where were the State fans last year when we won it all? Did they join the hoopla and rush around confessing that wow, wasn't that a great UNC-Georgetown game, and hey, how 'bout them Heels?

Of course not. They did what was expected of them as good fans. They sat home and sulked.

It is said that you can learn from your enemies. Let us learn from the Pack.

Remember, you are Tar Heels. You wear blue, not red. You love Carolina; you hate State. God is a still a Tar Heel. That place in Raleigh is still called Silo Tech, or if you prefer, Cow College.

The Wolfpack, although it wears the national crown, is still the Wolfpack.

It is time for true blue UNC fans to get off the Wolfpack bandwagon and back down to earth.

State fans are rightly obnoxious in victory or defeat. The least we Tar Heel fans can do is follow their lead. They understand what a rivalry is all about.

Now I hope I won't have to speak to you about this again.

Time for 'Save the Male' Campaign

It was a morning like any of the hundreds that preceded it.

It was shortly after 7, and I was comfortably sitting in bed with a cup of freshly brewed coffee and the newspaper. I trust I don't have to tell you which newspaper.

Buck the Cat was taking his sunrise siesta in my lap, and the radio was babbling softly in the background. I remember that disc jockey Bob Inskeep's odd word that morning was "punctilious," the first one I recognized in months.

It was thundering and lightning and pouring rain outside, and the traffic past my house had a soft gentle splashy sound to it.

The basement was slowly filling with water, but I didn't care. I was content in my morning ritual. I had even remembered to bring my raincoat in from the car the night before.

Then I came across this quote: "I'm sure we'll be able to make males dispensable in the very near future."

SAY WHAT!

My outburst was out loud. Buck the Cat, himself a member of the soon-to-be-useless male gender, shared my surprise and leaped to his feet. That made the waterbed undulate, which in turn made the precariously balanced coffee cup tilt past the point of no return, spilling the last swallow of coffee into my lap.

Thank goodness the coffee was lukewarm, but if what Dr. Clement L. Markert of N.C. State University says is true, it wouldn't have made any difference if it had been boiling.

Dr. Markert says that one day soon women will be able to have babies without participation by men, if you know what I mean and I'm sure you do.

And he's talking about no participation by men at all, either in person or in absentia. It wasn't too clear how it would work, but it has something to do with salt.

Then came the clincher: not only will men not be needed to make babies, but all of the babies born by this new method of reproduction would be females.

On behalf of the males of species, thanks a lot, fellow.

Now I know how the passenger pigeon and whooping cranes feel. I am a member of an endangered species.

The Save the Male campaign begins today, and I trust you will sign up.

Look at it this way. Passenger pigeons disappeared many years ago, and although I am sorry they're no longer with us, it really hasn't changed my life very much. I mean, a flock of 10,000 passenger pigeons coming over your house would make a real mess of your car.

The same thing applies to the whooping crane. There aren't many left, but I don't notice much of a difference. The lights are still bright on Broadway.

But men?

Imagine a world — shudder, shudder — without men.

Worldwide sales of chili powder, Tabasco sauce and jalapeno peppers would plummet, throwing millions of women out of work. There is not a woman alive who has not uttered those fateful words every time her man cooks up a pot of chili: "It's too hot."

Drive-in movies have had it. What could be more useless than a bunch of women sitting at a drive-in watching a John Wayne film festival?

Imagine sitting by a fire with your arm around your honey bunch, sipping on a drink and whispering sweet nothings. The fire crackling, and the ice is tinkling. Wonderful picture, isn't it?

Now take away the man.

There would be no fire. Women can build fires if pushed, but don't really like to do it, especially the part about going out to the woodpile and fighting the spiders and bugs to bring in the wood.

And the drink. Goodbye mellow bourbon reflecting the flames and hello gooey raspberry daiquiri. The melodic tinkle of ice would be replaced by the irritating whir of a blender.

And the sweet nothings? What can a shaker of salt say that any woman would want to hear? And goodness knows, men sitting by fires with drinks in their hands will tell a woman any foolish thing she wants to hear.

What you'll have is a bunch of women drinking colorful concoctions in a well-lighted place (to show off their new dresses) surrounded by healthy ferns. Let Norman Rockwell paint a picture of that.

And what are these salt-women of the future going to look like? That silly child with the umbrella on the salt box?

A baby's first words have traditionally been "da-da." What will they be now, "sodium chloride"?

There will be radical changes in your lives, ladies. Forget putting ketchup on your french fries. Who is going to open the ketchup bottle when the black gook around the top turns hard and unyielding?

No men, huh?

I'm sure many women out there are perfectly willing to give up the man they have now, but are women ready for a world without Tom Selleck, Rick Springfield or Matt Dillon? Dillon is not the one on Gunsmoke, guys, he's the other one. Oh forget it, just ask a woman.

Sure, men leave socks scattered around the bedroom and the washcloth in a sodden mess in the shower and little tiny whiskers in the sink. OK, so we tend to sit around the house on weekends, drinking beer straight out of the can and watching ACC basketball and ogling the cheerleaders.

But isn't total elimination of all men a bit drastic?

Save the Males. Take a male to lunch today.

Prisoner of the Techno-Generation

I always have considered my self a draft dodger in the Computer Revolution.

No thank you, I said to all those home computer advertisements and commercials. I am sure that your machines will do all you say they will do, but I don't need it done.

I don't need a $2,500 computer to help me balance my household budget. If I blew that kind of bucks, I wouldn't have a household or a budget. My system of home economics works fine: If I have money, I spend it. If I don't have money, I don't spend any.

But I'm not so sure anymore. I think my status has changed from draft dodger to prisoner of war.

My television set is hooked to a cable that lets me receive 18 channels. You television addicts out there with a coat hanger festooned with foil strips hooked to the back of your 12-inch black-and-white need not feel envious. There is nothing to watch. Now, it just takes me longer to make the decision to read a book.

But there is one thing I do like. I like that remote control thingamajig that lets me sit in my chair and change channels. Mine is called an Addressable Space Command, and it is terrific.

I was sitting there watching a basketball game, and during a timeout, I decided to scope out the latest rock video on my 24-hour rock video channel. Now, there's something we all need, bad music by ugly people.

I pushed the appropriate button, and nothing happened. I pushed and pushed, and nothing happened. I still was looking at the smirking face of Al McGuire. Boy George would have been better.

Then I looked down at my Addressable Space Command.

I was trying to change channels with my pocket calculator.

For a fellow who has consciously tried not to get caught up in all this, I am surrounded by high tech. And I don't mind.

Take my watch (No, this is not a Henny Youngman joke).

After years of swearing I would never own a digital watch, I bought one six months ago for the princely sum of $12.50. I bought a digital because it was the cheapest watch in the drugstore.

It tells me the hour, the minute, the second, the date, the day of the week, the month and the year. It is made entirely of plastic, runs on a battery about the size of a wart, and in six months, it has lost less than 30 seconds.

I was impressed enough that my watch knew the difference in months with 30 days and 31 days. That's pretty clever, I thought. Then it was New Year's Eve, and I'll be darned if that little sucker didn't know it. At the stroke of midnight, it not only changed the time, the day and the month, but it changed the year to 1984.

But I knew as sure as I'm sitting here that come Feb. 29, 1984, I'd have it by the short microchips. No way could my $12.50 plastic watch know that 1984 was leap year. I mean, what kind of demented brain would program a cheap watch to do something every four years?

It came to be Feb. 28, and I sat up until midnight to see what the watch would do. Would it say, "Hey, microchips, this is the end of February" and launch me into March a day early? Or would it decide that all months have 30 or 31 days and keep going?

The watch quietly rolled over to Feb. 29.

Ah ha, I said. Gotcha. You don't know this is a short month.

On Feb. 29, I sat up until midnight again. The human race was going to win one over the computer.

The seconds ticked off. it was 11:59 and counting.

Midnight.

My $12.50 plastic watch knew it was leap year. Half the people on Earth forgot, and my plastic watch remembered.

But I hate computers and high tech, I said, as I sat there admiring my smart watch. Or do I?

This column was written on something called a Digital VT 20/B. I can eliminate letters, words, lines, paragraphs or entire columns with the push of a button. Some have suggested I use those buttons more often, but I ignore them. I can move paragraphs from one place to another. It has a typewriter keyboard and a television screen, and I wouldn't think of pounding out a column on a typewriter anymore. And we're getting ready to get a new computer system that will make this one look like stale bread. I can't wait.

My car has a sensor that tells me if a taillight burns out or if any door is not completely closed, and a light comes on when I have two gallons of gas left in the tank. I like that.

I can make telephone calls around the world without ever

talking to an operator. OK, so I have to punchh 25 buttons in sequence to do it, but it sure is handy. My telephone also lets me call a number, and if the number is busy, I can tell my telephone to keep trying, and when the line is free, it will put the call through and then call me back to tell me. I like that.

I wouldn't think of trying to balance my checkbook without a pocket calculator. Yes, I know that 9 times 8 is 72, but my pocket calculator doesn't have to stop and think about it.

I have not gone to microwave ovens yet, but when I'm standing in the kitchen holding frozen lasagna in my hand, and it says I have to cook it 45 minutes in the oven or four minutes in the microwave, and I'm hungry enough to start gnawing on the frozen noodles, I must admit a microwave has crosssed my mind.

I've got a blender that knows the difference betwteen "beat" and "whip," and I sure don't, and it makes a great hollandaise sauce.

My thermostat keeps the room the same temperature all the time, the tape player in my car will skip over songs I don't like and automatically stop at the next tune, my clock radio wakes me up right on time and then shuts up when I go to work.

Now I'm waiting to see if my $12.50 plastic watch knows about daylight-saving time. The scary thing is, it just might.

State Seal a Big Deal — Maybe

Look folks, we've got a lot of out-of-staters coming in to North Carolina for our 400th birthday bash, so we need to look our best.

The first thing we'd better do is take our hallowed Great Seal and stick that boy in Secretary of State Thad Eure's glove compartment until the festivities are over. Put it way in the back, behind the road maps and the little packages of ketchup.

I do not want to be the one who has to explain to our visitors why that woman is holding that hat on that tobacco stick.

You may not, right off the top of your head on a Monday morning, be able to picture our Great Seal. That will teach you to stay home Sunday night like you ought to.

It is a round thing with the words "The Great Seal of the State of North Carolina" written around the edge of the circle from the lower left to the lower right with the words "Esse Quam Videri"

— which means either "To be rather than to seem" or "Pass the hushpuppies," I forget which — across the bottom.

Whatever it means, it is in Latin, a language not spoken anywhere I've ever been. And I've been around. I know they don't speak Latin in Latin America. I hear it came from Rome, but they speak Italian there.

Anyway, in the middle of the Great Seal is this picture of two women. One of them is standing up, and she's got this stick in her hand with a hat on top of it. In her other hand, she's got a scroll with "Consti Tution" written on it. She is wearing a nightgown with a beach towel draped across a shoulder.

The other woman is sitting on something. You can't tell what it is, although it could be a drink crate. She's holding a cornucopia by the tail, and all sorts of groceries are coming out the fat end, but I don't think there is a decent mess of collards or snap beans in the pile. There seems to be too much squash and not nearly enough onions for my taste.

The seated woman is holding three yard weeds in her hand and seems to be offering them to the standing-up woman who is not looking at the weeds at all, but keeping her eye on the squash.

Sneaking up behind them is a ship, and nearby are some mountains.

This may be good, Great Sealwise, but it sure flunks georgraphy. It is a right long hike from the beaches of Manteo to the mountains of Murphy.

Up at the top, just above the hat on the stick is "May 20, 1775." That is supposed to be when they signed the Mecklenburg Declaration of Independence, which you may have noticed comes about a year before the Big One on the Fourth of July up in Philadelphia and, therefore, is a Significant Moment in Our History. Never mind that not too many historians outside the city limits of Charlotte put much stock in the Mec Dec, because some clerk wrote it from memory 20 years later.

Why is it that if the woman sitting down has got this big thingamajig full of groceries spilling down at her feet, she is offering the standing-up woman nothing but three yard weeds?

Is she trying to make a deal for the hat on the stick? And why are these women dressed in nightgowns?

Another thing. Have these women been working out in one of those Yuppie spas? Their figures have certainly slimmed down over the years.

Although we are in more sexually liberated days, the women

who used to be on the Great Seal flashed a lot more skin than they do now. Of course, they had a lot more to flash.

We have a long history of Great Seals. The first one had two Indians on it. One of the Indians was a woman, and she was topless with one baby having dinner and another tugging on her skirt.

The Hat on The Stick shows up on Seal II, along with the ship and a map of the state, and our two women are there bringing supper to some king.

By Seal III, the woman with the food has taken a seat, and the other woman has taken off most of her clothes. The ship is much closer to the land. In fact, it almost has run up on the bank. The king is looking down the food-woman's dress.

Seal IV is a two-parter. The king and the ship are gone. (Maybe he was on the ship that ran up on the bank). One of the women has been drafted and is wearing a helmet (with her civilian hat still on the stick), and on the other side, the woman with the food is pointing at a cow and standing barefooted in a pasture.

Seal V is pretty racy stuff. The woman with the food looks like she's been rode hard and put up wet. Her hair is a real mess, and her dress has slipped off one shoulder exposing portions of herself. Both of them are barefooted, the seated woman is showing a lot of cleavage, and she has thrown her helmet away. But she still has the hat on the stick.

I don't know what was going on on Seal V, but Seal VI shows that both women have gained a whole lot of weight. And the ship that ran up on the bank on Seal IV is back way out at sea where it belongs. In fact, it may be leaving. The women seem saddened.

Seal VII is pretty close to what we have today. The women still are porkers. The woman with the hat on the stick has another hat on her head besides the one on the stick, which must belong to the grocery woman. And not only is the ship gone, the entire ocean is missing.

Seal VIII is the official Great Seal of today, adopted in 1971. What they did was take the woman's hat off, leaving her with just the one on the stick, put the ocean and the ship back, trim about 40 pounds off the women, fix their hair, lengthen one's skirt and put shoes on the other one and make them right cute.

Some archaeologist 10,000 years from now is going to have a fit with that hat on the stick.

Shocking State of the Cuisinart

Bubba palmed the steering wheel of the GMC with his right hand while his left hand slapped the drum rhythm against the door. He pulled into the dusty parking lot of the Way Out Yonder Saloon just as Z.Z. Top hit the last hot licks of "Sharp Dressed Man."

He strolled over to where his brother's BMW was parked and gave him a friendly wave as he got rid of that worn-out chew of Red Man.

His brother, the one they call Yuppie, pushed his Ferrari sunglasses up on his head and hit the button to turn off his Michael Jackson tape and another one to close the automatic sun roof. Dust is murder on good leather seats.

"Come on in, boy," Bubba said, as Yuppie checked one last time to make sure the bag of Brie was sitting in the shade. "They won't bite you." Yup wasn't so sure.

They walked to the door in silence, both thinking the same thing. What went wrong? How did one brother end up a Bubba and the other end up a Yuppie?

"What'll you boys have?" Darlene asked while she automatically reached for a cold Bud for Bubba. She was really looking at Yuppie when she said it.

"I'll have a Perrier spritzer with a twist," Yuppie started to say, but Bubba's elbow to the ribs stopped him just in time. Bubba told Darlene that Yuppie would have a Miller.

They sat down at a table, and Bubba looked long and hard at Yuppie while he tilted the can back and drained it.

"Boy, you look a little peaked," said Bubba.

"I think I've got it," said Yuppie.

"Got what?" said Bubba.

"I think I've got That Mecklenburg Thing," said Yuppie.

"Say what?" said Bubba.

"The Eddie Knox disease," said Yuppie. "He said in the paper that the reason he lost the runoff against Rufus was that he had That Mecklenburg Thing. I live in Charlotte, and it could be catching."

"Well, how do you know you have it?" said Bubba. "Heck, it could be just a green pasta allergy. That stuff gives off dust that irritates my sinuses something terrible."

"No, it's worse than that," said Yuppie, mentally making a note to get his Cuisinart blades sharpened. The last batch of pate had been a little lumpy, and Babs hated lumpy pate. But then, doesn't everyone?

"I think I really have it. I've had this incredible urge lately to go to Atlanta. I trade condos every six months and unless my office is at least 22 floors up, I feel insecure. And everybody hates me."

"What you've got is not a disease at all," said Bubba. "That Mecklenburg Thing is just the cold realization that everybody in North Carolina outside Mecklenburg County hates Charlotte. I know that comes as a surprise to you, but it's a fact. You'd better learn to live with it. Have another Miller."

"But why do people hate Charlotte so much?" said Yuppie, wondering why Darlene had not brought him a pilsner glass for his beer. "It is a vibrant, dynamic city, just like Atlanta. It has pretty, tall buildings made out of glass that you can't see through, just like Atlanta. It has a lot of lovely condos and neat-o places to live, just like Atlanta. You can buy Burberry coats all over town, just like Atlanta, and we have more quiche restaurants than barbecue joints, just like Atlanta. And the fern bars, why they're on every corner. Just like Atlanta."

"Let me put it as nicely as I can," said Bubba. "You could take Charlotte and set the place down in any state in the U.S. of A. and nobody would know the difference. The town ain't got no sense of place. Charlotte is about as Southern a city as Des Moines. The only thing most people in Charlotte think is wrong with Charlotte is that it ain't Atlanta.

"Now Brother Yup, North Carolina is a Southern state, like it or not. We talk Southern, we eat Southern, we look Southern. We're perfectly willing to accept folks from other parts of the country, and we expect them to be different. Heck, that makes them interesting. But we expect people from Charlotte, which is still in North Carolina, to be like the rest of us. Southern. Y'all seem ashamed to be Southern.

"Charlotte puts on airs, and if I have to tell you what that is, it may be too late.

"Don't get me wrong. There are some fine folks in Charlotte. Y'all got some good stuff out there, and Eddie Knox is a fine man, probably would have made a good governor. But y'all can't go around saying how wonderful you are all the time and not expect some of the folks outside Charlotte to get a little tired of it. Nobody likes folks who brag all the time. And frankly, some of us don't think Atlanta is all that hot, and it is not exactly the pattern we'd use to sew us a city."

Yuppie sat there stunned. It had never occurred to him that everybody didn't love Charlotte like he did. It was so high-tech and shiny and so '80s that he figured everyone envied it and wanted to live there. He was so proud of Charlotte, and it hurt him to hear what Bubba had to say.

Darlene had been listening to the conversation. She was touched by Yuppie's obvious discomfort. She leaned over and put her hand on Yuppie's shoulder.

"There, there," she said. "Don't take it so hard. I happen to know where you can get a nice quiche not three miles from here. Go have some; it'll make you feel better."

"Do they have white wine in bottles without screw tops?" Yuppie asked. "Do they have ferns and natural wood and everything? Just like Atlanta, er, Charlotte?"

"Sure they do, honey," said Darlene.

Bubba could have killed her.

"I feel much better now," said Yuppie. "You may hate us now because we're Charlotte and you're not, but it looks like to me you're heading in that direction, too. One day the whole state will be just like Charlotte. Won't that be wonderful? Then there won't be That Mecklenburg Thing anymore. Ciao, baby."

Yuppie drove off, the sound of his Culture Club tape lingering in the dusty air.

Bubba sat there sullenly. He knew Yuppie was right.

"What's the matter honey, somebody lick the red off your candy?" asked Darlene.

"Shut up, Darlene, and play me some Hank Junior on the juke box," said Bubba. "Play 'If Heaven Ain't a Lot Like Dixie' before it's too late."

Advice on Surviving a 40th Birthday

Today is Columbus Day, but I don't care. I have more important things to think about.

This is my first full day as a grown-up, 40-year-old person.

That statement will bring three reactions. The really ancient, decrepit old folks out there, those aged relics in their 50s, will say "Forty, huh? Big, fat, hairy deal." They have forgotten.

Those young, immature whippersnappers in their 30s will say, "Forty, huh? Big, fat, hairy deal." They have no vision of the future. It won't happen to them.

But there is another group, those in their late 30s who will cringe and say: "Here, you wanna read this? I gotta go to work." They do not wish to be reminded of their fate.

It is a popular myth that all birthdays ending in zero are somehow more important than others. That is not so.

The first biggie birthday comes at 13, when children become teenagers and begin talking back to their parents, growing pimples, hiding things in their rooms and acting sullen.

That is followed by 16, when they begin acting wonderful, for a week, so gullible parents will think they are mature enough to get a driver's license and take the family heap out for a few rounds of Death Race 2000.

Then is 19, when those smiling cherubs you have raised begin swilling down beer like steelworkers and chasing members of the opposite sex with crazed determination in their beady little eyes.

Twenty-one is important because the little ones overnight become adults. A laughable notion, but that's the way it works. At 20, they are kids. One day later, they are serious, responsible adults who begin hanging around liquor stores hoping they will be carded so they can flip out those IDs with practiced indifference.

Thirty comes next — notice how the interval between biggie birthdays is increasing — when the people in their 20s come face to face with reality. They get a whiff of the grave and begin that most hopeless of endeavors, taking stock of themselves and where they are going. If they are unmarried, they become desperate for wedded bliss. If they are married, they become sure life is passing them by. If they have a good job, they become bored. If they have a bad job, they become despondent.

Ah, but then comes 40. More jokes are made about turning 40 than all other ages combined, and they are all very funny.

Jack Benny made a living of staying 39 forever. Jerry Lee Lewis made a bundle with a record called "Thirty-Nine and Holding."

Some lyrics, "He's 39 and holding, holding everything he can, from 17 to 25 to prove he's still a man."

I have considered all the alternatives and decided that reaching 40 is terrific.

No longer do I have to wonder if I have, in fact, reached middle age. I have. No doubt about it.

Some people who are afraid of age claim that middle age comes about 55. That would be true if people lived to be 110, but since I can count on roughly 75 to 80 years (how we middle-aged folks dream and delude ourselves), 40 is smack dab middle age.

I wondered how I ought to mark this momentous occasion in my life. My friends and family got together and staged an Irish wake for me, complete with casket. Wasn't that sweet?

I thought about getting my hair cut real short, shaving my beard, buying a lime-green, double-knit leisure suit with contrasting stitching and joining a men's club, but I came to my senses in the nick of time.

The problem was that I felt compelled to live up to the legend of a middle-aged crazy who tries to hang on to his now-fled youth. I mean, it was expected of me. How could I disappoint my friends by behaving in a normal, rational manner? They were determined that I would have a midlife crisis or they would bloody well know the reason why.

So I made them happy.

I went out and bought the biggest, meanest, blackest, most chromed motorcycle in the world.

I bought a Harley-Davidson — 1340 cubic centimeters of screaming death.

My friends and family are so happy with my motorcycle. They take great delight in chuckling knowingly when they see it.

"Yep, he's 40 now and going crazy. You know how they are at that age," they say to each other when I'm not around.

To me, they smile as if I were a simpleton and say, "You must be turning 40."

The males of my acquaintance go home and tell their females about my motorcycle. They both have a good laugh about it, and the females usually say, "I don't know what gets into some men when they get to be 40."

I am so happy that my 40th birthday has brought such pleasure to my friends.

So men, when you turn 40, do something unexpected. Buy a motorcycle, take up skydiving, grow a beard, whatever it takes to make your friends happy. They will be so disappointed if you don't.

This is possibly your last chance to do what you've always wanted to do but were afraid to because of what people would say. Now you can get away with anything, and folks will smile.

You'll hear all the expected jokes, and you can laugh along with them and have a great time.

Then you can climb on your bad motorcycle and roar off, leaving them all with envy in their eyes. And you'll have the last laugh.

Turning 40 is the best opportunity for self-indulgence you'll ever have.

I wouldn't have missed it for anything.

Sam Slimy and the Phonegate Case

Tarboro

It was sunny in Eastern North Carolina. I was working the day watch in missing persons when I got a call for help from a lady who said she was Susan Wellborn of Plymouth: "Perhaps with your connections you can get to the bottom of the Diggerhole mystery."

The name is Slimy, Sam Slimy, and I'm a private eye.

It would be a tough case, but aren't they all when you're the best in the business?

Little did I know that when I was through I would have uncovered a dark conspiracy I like to call "Phonegate."

It started with a call to Alan Sykes, the mouthpiece for Carolina Telephone & Telegraph Co. He sounded nervous when I told him I was coming to pay him a friendly visit. He'd heard of me. He knew I was tough. I let him sweat into the phone.

I parked my heap outside Sykes' fancy office and kicked open his door just to get his attention.

"Why'd you do that?" he whined. "It was open. All you had to do was come in."

I told him to shut up and sit down. I hobbled over to a chair — the door was pretty tough, too — and pushed my battered fedora back on my head, lit a cigarette and watched the smoke curl to the ceiling before I spoke.

"OK, wise guy, where are you keeping Zack Diggerhole and Selma Davis?" I snarled. "I want answers and I want them now."

You could see the fear in his eyes. He lit a Marlboro with shaking hands and pretended that he didn't know what I was talking about. They all try that while they stall for time.

I decided to make it easy for him.

I told him about Zack Diggerhole and how Zack was listed in the telephone book in at least 28 North Carolina towns. I even read him the list:

Williamston, Columbia, Creswell, Hamilton, Plymouth, Windsor, Wake Forest, Fuquay-Varina, Clayton, Clinton, Garland, Newton Grove, Roseboro, Fayetteville, Parkton, Kinston, LaGrange, Grifton, Moss Hill, Pink Hill, Morehead City, Beaufort, Newport, Smithfield, Clayton, Four Oaks, Princeton, and Whiteville.

I told him that in each of those towns, Zack Diggerhole was listed as living at 122 E. James St. and his phone number was listed as 555-3001.

I also told him that in most of those towns there wasn't a St. James Street, east or west.

Then I told him about Selma Davis and how she was listed in at least 27 towns and, guess what, her address was listed as 122 E. St. James Street, and her telephone number as 555-3001.

"I thought we'd gotten rid of Selma," Sykes said. His answer gave me hope. Maybe I was in time. My foot was turning purple.

Then he made a mistake. They always do.

"Do you know about Tim Sadsuch?" he said.

I was cool. I'd heard rumors about Sadsuch, but this was the first time I'd gotten a name to go with the whispers I had picked up in the alleys.

"Yeah, I know it all," I told him. "Why don't you come clean? Who are Zack Diggerhole, Selma Davis and Tim Sadsuch, and what goes on at 122 E. St. James Street?"

Sykes was speechless, so he called in Mike Pittman. Pittman and I had worked together before, and he knew there was no use pretending with me. The jig was up, and he let it all spill out in a rush of words.

He told me, trying to laugh it off, that Zack, Selma, and Tim were not real people. He said they had been made up by the telephone company to protect their copyrighted telephone directories.

Pittman said telephone companies put fake names in the directory. If someone reprints the telephone book without permission, the phone company can prove the bad guys copied it because they included the fake listings.

"Selma Davis is a real person," Pittman said. "She works in our listing department, and when we were advised a few years ago to include fake listings, we used her name. And the address 122 E. St. James St. is the address of our operations department here in Tarboro.

"We've been replacing her name with Tim Sadsuch in the new directories."

I guess he expected me to fall for such an old gag.

I guess he expected me to believe that there are thousands of people out there bootlegging the phone book. I know I've thought about it, and I'm sure you have, too.

I can see it now. You go into a dimly lit barroom, and there, in the back booth, his face hidden in the shadows, a man with a foreign accent says, "Pssst, hey Mac, wanna buy a hot phone book?"

Pittman admitted that no one ever tried to bootleg the Carolina Telephone book, but he claimed he'd heard about it happening somewhere else. Indiana or somewhere, he thought.

I smiled through the mist of pain. Sure, Mike. Bootlegging phone books. Indiana. Right.

Guys in my business know that once you get them to confessing, they can't stop. They want to get it all off their chest.

"You want a tip?" Mike said, trying to get on my good side.

I massaged my swollen foot and didn't say anything. I don't make deals.

"In the Jacksonville phone book that is coming out in April will be the name Ivan Phosphor," he said. "Ivan will come right after the listing for the Phone Shop, so if someone misdials, they won't be bothering a customer."

I had one last question. Who came up with such flacky names? I knew the answer even before he spoke.

"It was a committee," Mike said.

Wouldn't you know it.

I limped back to my heap, my foot throbbing gently. Another case was solved.

Sam Slimy wins again.

Coast to Capital on N.C. 50

It begins as South Anderson Boulevard on the southern end of Topsail Island.

It is N.C. 50, not a major road, but one that can show off the best of Eastern North Carolina.

It is a road of gentle curves through a verdant farmland, a meandering little country road that never presumes to be more. It does not rush, it ambles.

If you want to see that the farms, fields, pines and towns of Eastern North Carolina can be stunning in their simple beauty, take this road.

Ride with me on my favorite road from the barrier islands to Raleigh.

There once were plans to turn Topsail Island into a site for rocket tests. Landowners thought there was more money to be made on tourists. The rocket tests were moved to Florida to a swamp called Cape Canaveral. The test site could have been here. Only a few observation towers are left.

Holly Ridge, on the mainland and a boomtown during World War II, is only a wide spot in the road now. Nearby Camp Davis, which was built, used and razed all within five years, is a pine forest. A few chimneys peak through the trees, there are overgrown roads if you look carefully, and back in the woods is an airstrip used by the forest service, the Marines and drug smugglers.

The road cuts like a chainsaw swath through the logging woods. All you see are mile after mile of trees, cut-over fields and logging trucks.

At 25 miles, the world's most isolated ice cream war is being waged between Davis Variety and the R-Mart across the road. Both brag they're all hand-dipped.

Then the road gets ugly. Mile after mile of rusted, broken-down trailers and battered homes squat by the road as you approach Maple Hill.

A bright blue-and-white revival tent, with the sides rolled up and chairs in neat rows, sits next to the St. Paul Holy Church, waiting for the hot sun to go down and the hotter preaching to begin.

It gets prettier and tobacco starts near Chinquapin, and suddenly you know you're in Duplin County, produce basket for the world. There are cukes and peppers growing so fast you can almost see it.

The lovely old Chinquapin Presbyterian Church is straight ahead. There you turn left.

Now you're in chicken country, house after house proclaiming proudly they grow chickens for Nash Johnson, the chicken king of Rose Hill.

There are more curves here than a stadium full of cheerleaders, but it is a good, smooth road where old men still sit in front of general stores and wave as you go by.

As 62 miles turn over on the odometer, you come to Kenansville, a pretty town. There to the right is the restored Duplin County Courthouse, farther on Liberty Hall and the Graham House Inn. Kenansville is particularly pretty at Christmas, when the whole town puts candles in the windows.

N.C. 50 joins N.C. 24 for the fast run to Warsaw. On the right you pass the Country Squire, a place where you can get a 72-ounce steak free — if you can eat every bite of it.

And you pass Westwater Hams, where Henry West cures hams in a swamp he turned into a paradise. Visitors by the hundreds visit Henry's gardens every spring.

On the left, 70 miles after the beginning of the journey, is the Twin States Exxon where Warsaw people go into mourning when the Tar Heels lose a basketball game and go crazy when they win.

A couple once won a free trip to Warsaw as a joke because the name sounded funny. They quit laughing when Warsaw put out the red carpet and showed the couple the time of their lives.

If all else fails, you can drop by the hardware store and listen to Jimmy Strickland tell stories about outhouses.

The next leg of the trip, up N.C. 50 and U.S. 117 is no fun. It is an industrial strength highway, a favorite of trucks hauling chemicals from the Wilmington port.

But the last segment lasts only eight miles and you're in Faison, home of Cates Pickle Co., more vegetables than you've ever seen and the Faison Produce Market on the northern outskirts of town. Millions of dollars change hands here every summer in this deceptively simple looking series of sheds.

Then it is back to the open country, and when you hit Sampson County, the state's largest, you know it. Here, the produce fields stretch to the horizon. You see the first migrant workers as you go through a crossroads where you find the Sutton Insurance Ageny, Sutton Used Cars, Sutton Supply Co., and Sutton's Inc.

You're in Suttontown.

Towns come faster now. Dobbersville, where three fat sheep graze in a front yard. Newton Grove, which has one of the few remaining traffic circles in the middle of town.

Then there is Benson, where on Sunday nights teenagers from surrounding counties meet in a ritual called cruising. Hundreds of cars jam the streets from late afternoon until dark, back and forth, cruising, flirting and driving motorists crazy.

The change is dramatic north of Benson. The soil goes from rich brown to sandy red at the 118-mile point, and you hit the first dramatic valley that signals you have left the flat Coastal Plain and are heading into the hilly Piedmont.

At 135 miles, there is Wimpy Williams' general store in Garner where you can buy anything that was ever made by the hand of man.

The fun is over at 137 miles when you hit U.S. 70 for the dash into downtown Raleigh. Don't look, just drive and try to stay alive.

But there is one nice thing left at 141 miles — a stunning view of the Raleigh skyline.

The Mysterious Beast of Bladen

Bladenboro

The swamps are dark at night — wet shadowy places where only a brave or foolish person would go.

"We all got a little crazy," Howard McDill said. "I wouldn't go back in there for anything now, but it was exciting then."

McDill, a retired plumber who lives near Fayetteville, last

walked in the swamps of Bladen County 30 years ago when he was part of the hunt for the legendary "Beast of Bladen."

He was young then, a hunter by avocation. When word spread that a monster was terrorizing the night near Bladenboro, McDill joined hundreds of farmers, service-station men, mill hands, professional hunters and drunken college students in a bizarre weeklong prowl in the swamps.

"It is a wonder we didn't all get shot," McDill said. "I've never seen so many guns in my life. But sure, we wanted to get that thing."

That thing was described by one man as sounding like "a woman with a knife stuck in her back" when it screamed. Others said it was a vampire panther, a bloodsucking wild thing that killed at least eight dogs and a rabbit in a weeklong rampage. More sensible people said it was probably a lost, hungry and frightened animal, probably a big cat or dog.

It began on the night of Dec. 29, 1953, when a 21-year-old housewife heard her neighbor's dogs whining and whimpering. She walked onto her porch near Clarkton, and in the darkness she saw the monster three houses away.

It looked like a big mountain lion, she said, and came right at her. At the last moment, she screamed, and her husband burst through the front door just as the big cat turned and ran.

Then the reports started coming in. Dogs were dying all across the county, their bodies drained of blood. Some were horribly mangled, the reports said, while others were merely opened and drained dry.

Two dogs on Woody Storm's farm were the first to die. Farmer Gray Callahan reported one of his dogs was dead, and then D.G. Pait said he watched from a service station as the beast caught a dog and dragged it howling into the woods.

The police were on the case. Professional hunters were brought in from Wilmington. Tracks were found near the woman's house, tracks that Police Chief Roy Fores said were bigger than a silver dollar.

Lloyd Clemmons was one of the few to see the animal and give a good description: It was about 3 feet long and about 20 inches high, with a 14-inch tail and a catlike face.

Some said it was a panther, but scientists said there were no panthers about. Then other scientists said there used to be panthers in the swamps, and perhaps this was the last of the litter. Others said it was a coyote or a feral dog. No one knew.

And no one cared. All they wanted to do was kill it.

"I read the paper," McDill said. "A bunch of us who hunted together took off down there with our dogs."

It was a mob. Estimates are that 500 armed men, some of them sipping on the stumphole whiskey for which Bladen was then justifiably famous, congregated in the town to hunt for the beast. Local officials considered calling in the National Guard, not to hunt the beast but to keep the crowd calm.

"I never saw a thing, but I was scared to death," McDill said.

"There were people yelling everywhere, hundreds of dogs barking, people shooting at anything that moved. Hell, if there'd been anything there, it would have died from laughing at us. We couldn't have found a bull elephant in those woods."

The stories got wilder. Expert trackers said it appeared there were two creatures traveling together. Somebody found a rabbit with its head bitten off. Blue-tick hounds were staked in the woods as live bait while their hunter-owners hid nearby. One bait-dog was killed, and nobody saw a thing.

But terror that intense cannot be sustained. Besides, the weather was turning colder. One night stumbling through the wet woods in January is enough to satisfy anyone's blood lust.

"We went that one night, and it was ridiculous," McDill said. "Then we went back on the weekend, and it got even worse. There were children playing everywhere, all these people with guns and dogs and the law trying to keep things organized. You couldn't even find a place to park."

The story reached its ridiculous climax when a gaggle of fraternity boys from Delta Kappa Epsilon at the University of North Carolina at Chapel Hill descended on the southeastern North Carolina town to find the monster. They were armed to the teeth with harmless youthful bravado and deadly shotguns.

That's when local officials announced that the hunt was over, the Beast of Bladen was no longer a threat and would everyone kindly pack and move out.

No more was heard from the Beast of Bladen. But one local man did find some good out of the whole thing.

He was quoted in the newspaper stories at the time as saying, "I hope they never catch it. Before the Beast came, my wife and I had twin beds."

They say you can still hear the call of the big cat in the swamps of Bladen on dark rainy nights when weird things always happen.

"He's probably still in there laughing," McDill said.

The Sons You Sent to War

Charles Van Gorder and John Rodda are best friends, business partners and — for more than 35 years — country doctors working side by side in the North Carolina mountain village of Andrews.

Theirs is a friendship forged in fire and tempered in ice. What they went through together makes most best friends sound like passing acquaintances.

"John Rodda caried me for 180 miles through the snow," Van Gorder said. "And then I carried him."

For almost a year, Van Gorder and Rodda went throught the worst the world can throw at two men. They were shot, pursued, captured, beaten, imprisoned, starved and frozen.

Through all that, they stayed together, as friends and doctors, taking care of each other and anyone they came across who needed their help.

The testing began in 1944. Van Gorder and Rodda, Army surgeons, volunteered for an experiment. They joined the 101st Airborne Division and volunteered to go into combat as front-line surgeons.

On the night of June 5, 1944, they blackened their faces, packed their medical bags and went in by glider as the 101st paratroopers landed seven miles behind German lines at Normandy, four hours before the D-Day landings began.

After crash-landing in a field, the doctors set up shop in an old castle, where three days of carnage began.

"We set up the first hospital treating the first casualties on D-Day," Van Gorder said during a recent visit to Raleigh. "The Army wanted to know if having surgeons on the front line with the Airborne would make a difference in casualties. Before, all casualties had to be evacuated for surgery.

"We had sterile packs for 75 operations. But we ran out of those immediately. By noon, we had 500 wounded outside. We operated on those we thought we could help."

For three days, they did not sleep. They stood on a bloody floor operating on wounded paratroopers. Putting patients on litters placed on top of medical cases, they operated around the clock, treating hundreds of wounded men.

"On the night of June 9, I was so exhausted during an operation that I fell asleep in the middle of surgery and my head slumped forward," Van Gorder recalled.

In August, they flew into battle with the paratroopers again, this time in Holland.

"One night, things got so bad I said I was only going to operate on left legs," Van Gorder said. "I said I had always wanted to specialize. That one night, I amputated 18 left legs."

The incredible story continued. In December, German forces began the biggest fight of the war, the Battle of the Bulge. Van Gorder and Rodda were in a rest area when the word came to head for Bastonge.

"We set up our hospital at a crossroads just outside Bastogne," Van Gorder said. "Rodda and I had a patient on the table when the Germans began firing into the hospital tent."

The hospital was surrounded, and the doctors were taken prisoner. Then began the long march through the worst winter of the war.

Van Gorder had been wounded by shrapnel. For 10 days, Rodda carried his buddy as they were marched father behind German lines.

"If he'd left me, I would have been shot," Van Gorder said.

They ended up in a German prisoner-of-war camp deep in Poland. By February, Soviet soldiers were near the camp, so the Germans ordered the prisoners to march back into Germany.

"We knew we were not going back into Germany, so one night we escaped," Van Gorder said.

Then began a remarkable odyssey across the battlefields of Europe. Without equipment or weapons, trapped between two warring armies, the surgeons strugggled to stay alive.

"One night, we were picked up by a Polish man in a three-seat bobsled," Van Gorder said. "We were riding along when a German woman sniper jumped into the back seat. She rode behind us for a mile."

Finally, they made contact with the Soviet army.

"We came around a corner, and there was a tank with the barrel pointed right at us," Van Gorder said. "A woman major crawled out and asked us if we would operate on Russian soldiers.

"We started operating, with a nun holding a candelabra for light. It was so cold that night that we had to put our hands down inside bodies of wounded men to warm them up enough to work."

It seemed that it would never end, that the two surgeons would never make it out alive. They were mistreated by the Soviets, who refused to feed them or let them ride on trucks.

"If if had not been for the Polish underground, we would have died," Van Gorder said. "They took us in and shuttled us from hospital to hospital, taking care of their wounded. We had been treated better by the Germans than we were by the Russians."

Trying to make it overland back to the U.S. Embassy in Moscow, the doctors made it to Brest Litovsk. There they met other Americans and former British POWs who had taken over a train. The train took them 1,600 miles across the Soviet Union to the port of Odessa, where a British ship picked them up and took them to safety in Naples.

After the war, Van Gorder visited his father in Andrews. He realized the mountain village needed him.,

"My idea was to start a little hospital and then move on," Van Gorder said. "I called Rodda and asked him to come down and join me. He said he'd come and stay until I got the hospital started, but he wasn't going to live in such a desolate place.

"That was 38 years ago, and we're still there."

Both doctors have retired, Rodda in 1978 after lung surgery and Van Gorder last year.

"Both of us would have been dead if it wasn't for the other," Van Gorder said. "Yes, he's my best friend."

Fighting Homefront Battles

New Bern

They call themselves The Group, and they are the sons you sent to war.

Jim Lafkas, 38: "We've been judged by television, not for the good things we've done but for the bad. Don't judge us, you weren't there, and you don't have the right."

Jack Nunn, 36: "If you tell them you're a Vietnam veteran, they shy away from you."

Allen Hutson, 33: "I can understand why they shy away from us. They are ashamed and embarrassed."

Gordon Commodore, 36: "For 13 years, I ran away from it with a bottle. I constantly drank myself into oblivion."

Clinton Morrow, 37: "The best part of the day was over when the alarm clock went off, that is if you'd been able to sleep."

Layers of gray cigarette smoke hung heavy in the closed room. People smoke more when they're tense.

The five men looked older than most men their age. The lines in their faces were deep. Their dark eyes were wary; anger flashed like summer lightning. The laughter, the few times it came, rang bittersweet and hollow. And the tears came, too, but without shame.

Their sanctuary had been invaded, and their instincts told them to be careful. They had no reasons to trust the stranger among them, but they tried.

"Six months, ago, if you'd walked into this room, these people would have run you away," said Patricia Hutson, Hutson's wife. "But we decided the story had to be told."

On Jan. 13, five Vietnam veterans and two of their wives gathered in the stuffy room in New Bern. They had lost the only person they had trusted in a long time.

There was a plaque on a coffee table. It read, "Dr. Alan F. Sonette — A true friend who helped us come home."

They wanted you to know that one man could make a difference. They wanted other veterans to know that there was help, but they had to look hard to find it sometimes.

Sonette, a psychiatrist with Neuse Mental Health Center, spent the last 18 months of his life helping these Vietnam veterans cope with what has come to be known as delayed stress syndrome.

It wasn't the first time most of the veterans had sought help. But they had not found it.

"You get sick of hearing there is no such thing as delayed stress," Commodore said.

"People say they don't believe in delayed stress syndrome," Morrow said. "That's like saying you don't believe in cancer."

Sonette believed. A former Army psychiatrist, he had seen doctor friends wracked by memories of the war. He knew that some men didn't leave all their battles behind when they got on that plane and left Saigon to fly home, to the place they call "the World."

But he was blazing new ground. The military had been proud of the fact that Vietnam fighters suffered much less of what in other wars was called shell shock and battle fatigue.

What the military did not know was that Vietnam's emotional distress would come later, after the war, when the men tried to forget it and come home. It would come to be called delayed stress syndrome, and it would be controversial. Some experts would say there was no such thing, that emotional problems that returning Vietnam veterans were having had nothing to do with the war.

But Sonette believed, and he wanted to help.

He told the men and their families they would have to trust him.

"Tell me, and I'll try to understand," he told them.

They took him at his word, and they told him all of it. They told him how they couldn't sleep at night, how they couldn't keep a job, how their marriages had fallen apart, how they drank too much, how they popped pills, how angry they were, how sometimes they felt like striking back with violence at the society that had sent them to war and wouldn't let them come home. And they told him that all of them had thought about suicide.

He listened and prodded in the weekly group sessions that were supposed to last 45 minutes but often went on for hours. He put them in the hot seat and made them open up.

And he did something else. He brought their wives into the group because he knew that entire families suffer when one member suffers.

"He never failed our trust," Mrs. Hutson said.

"We saw him care," Lafkas said.

Slowly it began to work. The veterans and their wives had found shelter from the storm.

"We're not well," Hutson said. "But it helps having people around you who have shared your experience, who know the torment and hell we've put ourselves through since Vietnam.

"It is not easy being in The Group. Sometimes, it destroys me for three or four days because it brings back things I've tried to forget.

"But it has brought me from being totally out of my mind to where I can cope with society.

"This was not just a job to Dr. Sonette. His life was the good of his group."

Sonette is dead, but The Group will go on. The work is not ended, and to let it end now would be unfaithful to his memory, a memory they treasure because of the things he taught them.

He taught them they were not crazy, that they were victims.

He taught them that there were people they could trust.

He taught them they were not alone, that they had each other, that they had The Group.

He taught them that they could come home.

A Soldier Denied His Rest

Bahama

The young soldier's grave lay undisturbed for almost 123 years. His service done, he rested in peace.

Then the grave robbers came, and now the bones of a young soldier who died in his first battle are scattered, some in the muck and water that fills his open grave, some perhaps carried off by wild things in the woods and some in the basement of a state office building in Raleigh.

Why would someone dig open a forgotten grave in a family cemetery? What would drive them to commit such a detestable violation of basic human dignity?

"They probably did it to get the buttons from his uniform," said Michael Hill, a researcher with the state Department of Archives and History, who pieced together the story of Preston Mangum. "They could be worth $300 each to a collector."

The grave robbers probably never heard of the young man whose grave they pillaged in search of loot. All they knew was that his name was William Preston Mangum, that he was 24 years old when he died of wounds suffered July 21, 1861, at the first Battle of Manassas. That much was written on his tombstone.

They never knew of the Bible in his breast pocket that almost, but not quite, saved his life. They never knew that he was the only son of one of Durham County's most illustrious men. They never knew how he died a hero's death, rallying his men to charge a federal position on the bloody battlefield of Manassas. They never knew how he suffered for seven days, dying in the end because there was not enough medicine or bandages or doctors to heal his wounds. They never knew that he was one of the very first North Carolinians to fall in battle.

All they cared about was the only thing William Preston Mangum carried to his grave, his Confederate lieutenant's uniform.

The young soldier was born in 1837 and was the sole male heir to the luxurious Mangum plantation called Walnut Hall, with its 600 acres of beautiful, rolling northern Durham County farmland. He was, Hill says, the "apple of his father's eye," and when he was 10 years old, he spent six months in Washington with his father, who served 20 years in the U.S. Senate and, at one time, was second in line to the presidency.

At age 18, he enrolled in the University of North Carolina, where his record is less than sterling. He lived in Room 12 of Old West dormitory, joined Delta Phi fraternity and in his sophomore year was absent from prayer 34 times, from "recitation" 26 times and from worship five times. He did not return to the university.

On May 1, 1861, 18 days after Confederate troops fired on Fort Sumter, Preston joined Company B, Sixth North Carolina Regiment, a unit known as the Flat River Guards. He received two shirts, two pairs of socks, two handkerchiefs, a flannel shirt, a coat and a blanket.

On June 30, because he was a good soldier and because his father was wealthy and a famous statesman, Preston was commissioned a lieutenant.

In late June or early July 1861, Preston made his last trip home before going into battle. His sister, Pattie, had given him a Bible to carry to war, but Preston wanted a smaller Bible to carry in his breast pocket. His sister passed on the request to a cousin, a minister named Adolphus Mangum. But the Rev. Mangum could not find a small Bible.

In July 1861, the Sixth was rushed north to meet federal troops heading south for Mannasas, Va. The battle, called the Battle of Bull Run by federal forces, was the first major battle of the war and one of the few major Confederate victories.

The battle had begun when the Sixth arrived at the front. They came upon a battery of artillery that was firing on Virginia troops and immediately opened fire and charged into the face of grapeshot.

The Rev. Mangum witnessed that charge. Later, he would write of Preston, ''When the charge was ordered, he bravely passed to the onset and with waving sword and thrilling voice, cheered and rallied the heroic column as it staggered before the fiery storm.''

Preston and his men captured the federal battery, and when it was over, as Preston leaned against a cannon to catch his breath and collect his thoughts after his first taste of battle, a musket ball slammed into his chest.

They ripped open his uniform and found a large wound in his chest. They also found a Bible torn by the musket ball, a large Bible he had carried stuffed in his jacket in place of the small pocket-size one he had asked his sister to buy.

The large Bible had deflected the ball from his heart, and instead of dying immediately, he was taken to the village of Louisa Courthouse, where every home had been opened as a temporary hospital. He was placed in the Methodist parsonage.

There was no medical equipment and no one to take care of the wounded soldier. The Rev. Mangum stayed by his side, doing what he could for seven days. But on July 28, riddled with gangrene, Preston died.

His body was returned to Walnut Hall, where his aged and sick father waited on the front porch of the mansion. Preston was buried in a family cemetery plot about 500 yards from the house where, in about six weeks, his father would be laid to rest at his side.

Preston wrote a short verse before the battle and left it in a notebook that was found in his belongings: ''In the summer land they've placed him, 'neath a sky that's ever blue. And heaven never smiled on one more generous or true.''

Now, 123 years later, that ''summer land'' became the hunting ground for grave robbers.

He deserved better than that.

Tribute to a Fallen Texan

Goldsboro

"We want to let it be known that as long as this Texan remains at rest in North Carolina, his Tar Heel cousins will take care of him," said Reid Tunstall.

"He represents the best of American character; to believe, to fight and to die for what is sacred."

And so the people of Goldsboro, as they have for more than a century, still honor a young Texas Ranger who died far from home.

His grave in Goldboro's historic Willowdale Cemetery is covered with yellow roses this Memorial Day, and his beloved Lone Star State flag hangs in the quiet summer heat. He was but one soldier who fell. But there is something special about Jared K. White from Austin County, Texas, something that has kept his memory alive through the years.

He represents every brave soldier who left home at age 19 to serve his country. He represents every brave soldier who gallantly fought for his cause, suffering the horror that is war. He represents every brave soldier who died, giving the last full measure of devotion to the people back home who were proud of him and grieved for him when he died. He represents every brave soldier who lies in a distant grave, his service honorably done. He is what Memorial Day is all about.

Jared K. White was 19 and a farm boy from West Texas when he joined the fabled 8th Texas Calvary, the brave band of hard-riding Texans who fought for four years as Terry's Texas Rangers. Their name was so honored that when the war was over, the first statewide law enforcement agency would take their name.

White and his fellow Rangers fought their way across the South from 1861 to 1865. When there was nothing left but the dream of the Confederate States of America, when Gen. Robert E. Lee was trapped by Gen. Ulysses S. Grant at Petersburg and Gen. Joseph Johnston was trapped by Gen. William T. Sherman at Goldsboro and the Confederacy was nothing more than a small slice of two battered states, Jared K. White was still riding hard in Eastern North Carolina.

The war would end three weeks later, but on March 20, 1865, on the banks of Nahunta Creek near Goldsboro, young White still had a job to do.

The Texas Rangers were on patrol near Goldsboro when four of them, including White, came upon a band of Union foragers stealing food from a young Wayne County mother who was at home alone with her child and a young servant girl.

The Rangers, as they always had done when faced by the hated "bummers," did not hesitate. They attacked and killed the foragers, looping ropes around boots and dragging their bodies behind their horses and dumping them in sink holes in the woods.

But one of the bummers was alive and escaped back to Union headquarters to report that the Rangers still were fighting in the area.

Sherman sent out a patrol to trap the Rangers, and the two sides met at Nahunta Creek near what is now Fremont.

A group of Union infantrymen were marching up a small road when they were attacked by the Rangers, who were lying in wait in Nahunta Creek. Another group of Union calvarymen rode up the creek itself, and in the first volley from the Confederate rifles, 14 of the Federals fell.

White repeatedly dashed from his cover to fire at the Federals, and on his last dash, he was shot to death in the saddle. Another Ranger, his horse killed by the same round that killed White, leapt into White's empty saddle, and the battle continued until the Federals withdrew.

His Texas comrades wrapped White's body in his horse blanket and buried him under a large oak tree on a hill overlooking the small and since-forgotten battlefield. They built a sturdy wooden fence around the grave and asked William Benjamin Franklin Fort, who owned the land where the battle and burial took place, and a slave named Durdin Fort to see that it was never disturbed. Durdin Fort was given the Ranger's saddle to seal the bargain.

William B. Fort, the elder Fort's son, wrote in 1904: "Oftentimes, while walking over the old homestead, I would wander by the Ranger's lonely grave beneath the whispering pines and wonder if the loved ones in far-off Texas would ever learn the fate of the dear soldier boy missed at the family fireside."

The war moved on from Goldsboro and Nahunta Creek, and three weeks later, it all would end for Lee at Appomattox and for Joe Johnston at Bennett Place near Durham.

The Texas soldiers who fought would be going home, and some of them would be passing the grave of their comrade left behind in Goldsboro.

Young Jared White was dead, but the century-old tradition that he inspired had just begun.

The war ended in spring 1865, and tens of thousands of Southern soldiers began the long, lonely trek home across a devastated Dixie. Many of them came past Goldsboro, where White had been buried.

William B. Fort, on whose farm the young Texas soldier fought, died and was buried, was concerned that his family in Texas know what had happened to him. In 1904, he recalled what happened:

"Fate soon solved the problem, as there came in the neighborhood two Texas soldiers on their way home down in Texas from Appomattox driving a double team to a buggy. Hearing of these Texas soldiers, I drove over to Nahunta and met them.

"I found one of them to be Colonel Hooks, who came by the Hooks neighborhood to visit some of his father's relatives, his father having years before emigrated to Texas.

"I informed Colonel Hooks of the death and burial of Ranger White. He said he knew White and his family as they were neighbors in Texas. The colonel said he would inform the White family upon his arrival home."

Months after Hooks made it back to Texas, Fort was sitting with his brother and father on their front porch one day when a buggy with two men drove into the yard. It was followed by a hearse.

One of the men was Jared White's brother. He had ridden a horse from Texas to North Carolina with instructions to make sure the dead boy was indeed Jared and, if so, to rebury him in the Confederate Cemetery in Goldsboro.

"All of us proceeded to the grave after taking along with us Durdin Fort, who had assisted in the burial of the ranger," Fort wrote. "When the body was exhumed after unfolding the army blanket from around it, his brother said he could swear to those two family rings upon his brother's fingers.

"Young White placed those rings in his pocket to show his parents that they were the same rings that were placed upon his dead brother's fingers when he left to join the 8th Texas Rangers.

"After placing the body in a beautiful casket, they carried it to Goldsboro and reburied it in a lot apart from the beautiful Confederate monument erected by the Goldsboro Rifles to the 800 Confederate heroes who bivouac beneath it.

"Young White had a marble slab erected at the head of his brother's grave and built a substantial iron railing around the grave. Before he left, he informed me that his father requested that our family should look after his hero son's grave."

That promise, made a century ago, has been honored.

For many years, well into this century, a ceremony was held each Confederate Memorial Day (May 10) at White's grave. A Texas flag was hoisted, the grave was covered by the yellow roses of Texas and a 21-gun salute was fired.

"I don't know when it ended," Reid Tunstall said as we stood by White's grave. "But eventually, they stopped having the ceremony.

"I was doing some research trying to identify the 800 unknown Confederate soldiers buried in a mass grave, and I came across the story of Jared White. I thought it would be a good idea to revive it."

Tunstall is active in Civil War re-enactment groups. In 1981, he and his friends again began honoring the young Texas soldier who died in Eastern North Carolina.

And so one Saturday, while most of us thought about picnics and summer, a band of Confederate soldiers in full uniform fired a 21-gun salute over the grave of Jared White. A gospel group sang a haunting, mournful version of "Yellow Rose of Texas." Yellow roses were scattered on the grave, still surrounded by the iron fence, and a new Texas flag was raised.

"The Texas flag flies year-round here," said Tunstall, planning director for Wayne County. "Each year, the Sons of Confederate Veterans in Texas sends us a new one, and we send the old one back to Texas with full honors.

"Here was a young man who rode 2,000 miles from home on horseback to fight for what he believed in. He fought side by side with Tar Heel boys, and I would like to think that if a Tar Heel boy died in Texas, the good people there would take care of him.

"As long as we live, this Texas boy will be taken care of."

Life and Death in the Pacific

Topsail Beach

It is hard to imagine anything more terrifying, but it happened so quickly that Lou Muery didn't have time to be scared.

'We were flying at 500 feet when the engine quit," Muery said. "We had just enough time to tighten our shoulder harness, turn into the wind and bring the tail down."

Seconds later, Muery's plane crashed into the Pacific Ocean. He and radioman Rick Ritcher scrambled into a life raft and watched as their plane slowly sank.

They were a long way from safety, and nobody knew where they were.

It was May 21, 1942, and Muery and Richter were returning to the USS Hornet from a 650-mile patrol over the vast Pacific.

"We were not permitted to call on the radio in case you went down," Muery said. "You did the best you could."

For 23 days — long days of sweltering in the blistering equatorial heat, long nights of shivering, suffering through storm, having no food and only the water they trapped during rainshowers and the soul-numbing isolation — the Navy fliers hung on to their lives and their sanity.

They took inventory when they got settled into the 4-by-7-foot bright yellow raft. They had a survival kit with emergency rations — mostly candy — for two days, two canteens of water, two aluminum paddles, a mirror, a set of signal flags and a hand pump to keep the raft inflated.

"We didn't eat any food at all for the first couple of days," Muery said. "We talked about how the Lord went 40 days and 40 nights without food, and we planned on lasting that long. In the late afternoon, we'd treat ourselves to a couple of malted milk tablets."

Muery and Richter knew that no one would look for them. There was a war on, and the lives of two fliers were expendable. It would have been senseless to stop a task force of ships to search for two men who didn't come back from a mission.

'We didn't try to row that first night," Muery said. "The next day, we tried to row in the direction we thought an island was. We might hit an island, but we realized we didn't have any idea where we were going.

"So we rigged a sail from our parachutes. The wind was

constant from the northeast. We didn't know where we were going, but at least we were moving. It made us feel a lot better.''

The days dragged by with a deadly sameness. It would be hot all morning until noon, when the wind stopped. Then it would be calm, the ocean glassy smooth. The homemade sail hung limp while the two men wrapped themselves in parachute silk and poured water over themselves to stay alive. Then it would be night, and it would get cold.

"You couldn't wait for the sun to go down, and you couldn't wait for it to come up again,'' Muery said.

After about a week, a storm hit. The high wind flipped the boat and destroyed what little food they had. There would be no more candy to celebrate living another day.

"The problem now was that the boat was upside down,'' Muery said. "We climbed up on the bottom of it and tried to turn it back over. We were so weak by then that we couldn't do it.

"But you get strength when you have to have it, and we pulled one last time and got it turned over. We climbed in it fast and got in the bottom and rode the storm out, huddling there in the bottom of the boat being thankful.''

The only thing that kept the men alive was water. It rained every couple of days, and the men used a cloth sling from the first aid kit to trap water in a metal box.

"You get over the hunger after two or three days,'' Muery said. "But you're always thirsty. I used to think a lot about milkshakes, anything you'd ever had that tasted good.''

Their spirits went up and down. They prayed a lot and kept each other going. When one wanted to quit, the other was there to urge him on for just another day.

And there were always the sharks, watching and circling and waiting for one of them to slip over the side.

It was the 17th night when the monster came in the dark.

It was a bright, moonlit night in the tropics. They could see a long way and were making good time with their homemade sail.

Muery was in the stern using the paddle as a makeshift rudder when the great white shark attacked.

"He took a liking to the paddle,'' Muery said. "He swam by it and tapped it when he passed. The next time he came by, I gave him a good bump on the nose.''

Then the monster surfaced. He was at least 18 feet long, almost three times the length of their tiny boat. He circled once or twice and then attacked — just like in the movies.

"He came barrelling in on us," Muery said. "He was determined to hit us, and he did, full speed. But the boat held. There was just a small rip in the bottom."

Things got worse and worse. They were covered with sores, awash in four inches of water in the bottom of the boat, hungry, tired, dehydrated.

Then it was the 23rd day. It would be their last day at sea.

"The sun came up that morning, and we realized it was the 23rd day," Muery said. "We both started saying the 23rd Psalm. Neither one of us could remember it all, but we stumbled over it. We kept repeating it, over and over.

"Then we realized that for some time we had been seeing something on the horizon. We hadn't seen or heard anything for 23 days, but we knew we were seeing what looked like an island, and we were heading straight for it.

"We stared at each other, and then we hugged and cried and waited."

It was land, the tiny island of Nui, but they were not safe. The real horror was yet to come.

"We could see that landing on the island was going to be dangerous," Muery said. 'There were huge waves breaking on the reefs, and we had to cross them in our little raft. The waves must have been 15 feet high, and I know Rick was petrified.

"You see, he couldn't swim."

The men pumped up their life jackets, tied everything down and waited as the tide brought them closer to the surf. They knew there was no way their little boat could ride safely through such a tempest.

"We tried to paddle around the island to find calmer water," Muery said. "But we realized we were using up what little strength we had left. All we were doing was holding off the beach to keep from going in.

"We had already traveled, I learned later, 850 miles in an open raft across the Pacific. If we had missed this island, it would have been another 850 miles to the next one.

"We looked at each other and said, 'We gotta do it, so let's do it.' We turned the boat toward the beach and waited."

The wait was not long.

The first wave rolled the raft over. The two weakened, starving fliers were dumped into the surf that pounded the offshore coral reef.

Muery, who knew how to swim, tried to hold onto his buddy. But the force of the second wave separated them.

"I was not concerned; I knew I could make it," Muery said. "But even with our life jackets on, the waves sent us to the bottom. I grabbed the coral and tried to keep from being washed back out."

Fighting to stay afloat and alive in the swirling water, Muery looked back and saw Rick, his flying buddy who had suffered for 23 days in an open boat with him, floating face down in the water.

"The boat was hung on some coral, and I dragged Rick up on it, and tried artificial respiration. I'd never heard mouth-to-mouth, so I did it the way we'd been taught. It was no good, but I kept working on him.

"Finally, I gave up and draped myself over his body and passed out.

"I came to a little later and walked to the beach and sat there and looked and thought and wondered."

Just before dark, Muery went back into the water and brought Rick's body ashore and buried it in a shallow grave on the beach. Then he turned the battered raft over and got in it and went to sleep, exhausted and alone on an island in the middle of the southwestern Pacific.

"The next morning I woke up and saw Rick floating face down in the lagoon," Muery said. "The tide had washed him back out. I went back out and got him again and buried him farther up in the trees. I said a little prayer over him as I had the day before."

Muery wrapped silk rags around his feet, which had been ripped open by the coral, and, using one of the boat paddles as a crutch, hobbled down the beach. He weighed less than 100 pounds, down from his normal 170 pounds.

"I was thirsty, and I saw drops of water were on some leaves," he said. "I started licking the water off the leaves."

But Muery was not alone on Nui. Two natives who lived on the other side of the island had come to his side to search for material for a dugout canoe. They saw the strange apparition on the shore and ran away.

They went back across the island and notified two New Zealand coast watchers who lived with them that the Japanese had landed.

One of the New Zealanders radioed the Allies that some Japanese had invaded, and then he ran into the woods.

The other one, an unarmed soldier, gathered a group of men to investigate.

"I didn't see them," Muery said. "One of them came up behind me with an ax ready to cut my head off, and the New Zealander said, 'What are you, a Jap?'

"I turned around and shouted, 'God, no!' "

After 24 days, Lou Muery was safe.

The natives climbed coconut trees and brought down green coconuts from which he drank milk. Then they carried him across the island to their village, where he lived for another 23 days until a supply boat arrived.

"They were simple, very happy, very compassionate people," he said. "They took very good care of me."

The boat that came to his rescue was on an espionage mission. It was a 90-foot sailing yacht that prowled the islands to resupply the coast watchers and gather intelligence on enemy movements in the Japanese-controlled waters.

The trip south to the naval base at Suva in Fuji took another two weeks, including 48 hours hiding in a fog bank to escape Japanese ships searching for them. After many more weeks at Suva, he left for the United States.

What did he do when he got home, when he crawled off the train, emaciated and wearing bits and pieces of whatever uniform he could find?

He asked his fiancee whether their wedding was still on.

It was. Louis and Mary Lou Muery have lived happily for 42 years. They're retired now, living in Topsail Beach.

A Time of War — A Time of Love

Morehead City

It was a time of love and war, a time of birth and death, a time when the world went crazy and two young people fell in love amid the ruins.

He was a Yank from Swansboro, and she was a lovely red-haired English girl. Their paths would cross in Nottingham, England, and for a golden summer in 1945, while the mightiest armies in history tore at one another with savage fury, the two fell in love, got married and had a baby girl.

But life is not a fairy tale, happy endings are not ensured, and young dreams don't always come true.

Eugene Yeager was a 22-year-old U.S. soldier. Maisie Jean Humphreys was a 20-year-old daughter of a Nottingham shopkeeper. They met as so many American boys and English girls did during those violent days. They were married, and on July 28, 1945, Jean Elizabeth Yeager was born.

But what should have been a moonlight-and roses finish of a tender story of wartime romance became a heart-rending tragedy, a tragedy that would haunt the young soldier and his daughter for 38 years.

"My wife died during childbirth," said Yeager, 61, a retired civil sevice worker. "My mother-in-law and I agreed that she would raise Jean. I left England in December of 1945 to come home. I haven't seen or heard from Jean since."

Jean Yeager grew up in Nottingham, not knowing her father or anything about him. Family stories told her he was a U.S. soldier who had gone home, and that was all she knew.

"My Gran would not talk about my father at all," Jean said by telephone from Nottingham. "Every time I mentioned him, she would shut up. She felt she had already lost one daughter, and she was afraid she would lose me, too.

"For 38 years I wondered about him."

There were a few letters to the United States from Jean's grandmother, all of them saved by Yeager.

"She wrote about once a year," Yeager said. "She always told me everything was fine. The last letter I got was in 1952, and there was a picture of Jean riding on a donkey."

But Yeager's letters to his daughter were not getting through. And he didn't know it.

"My Gran tore up every letter or picture he sent," Jean said. "She would not mention him. He even sent a visa for me to come visit, and she tore that up, too. All I had to remember him by were some old wedding photographs.

"I never tried to find my father because I didn't want to hurt my Gran. She went into a fit every time I mentioned him."

Yeager, back home, remarried and a father again, didn't know that the ties that bind a father and a daughter had been severed by Jean's grandmother.

"I figured Jean didn't get in touch with me all these years because she didn't want to," Yeager said. "She had her own life, and I though she liked things the way they were. She had that right, and I accepted it.''

The years went by, and Jean often wondered about her father. And he wondered about her, two people who should have been together but were not.

"I always wondered if he was alive," Jean said. "I wondered what kind of man he was, and I always thought that if anything ever happend to Gran, the first thing I would do is try to contact him.''

Her grandmother died a year ago, and Jean began her long, painful search. She didn't know how to find her father. All she knew was his name and that once he was from North Carolina. But he could have died. He could have never come back to North Carolina. He could be anywhere, and she felt lost.

Then the Nottingham Evening Post began writing articles about the 40th anniversary of D-Day and reported that many of the Yanks who had been stationed in the Nottingham area would be back for a reunion.

"I wondered if my father would be one of them," Jean said. "I thought there might be some hope.''

Jean contacted the Post which wrote about her dream of being reunited with her father after more than 38 years. A copy of that story was sent to The News and Observer by Alan Gillies, an acquaintance of Jean.

He knew Yeager was once from North Carolina and asked me to see whether I could find him. I made up my mind to try. I thought a father and a daughter ought to have a chance, even after 38 years.

I found Yeager after a long day of searching and talked to him by phone at his home. With his permission, I called Jean in Nottingham to tell her I had found her father, alive and well.

Laughing and crying at the same time, she said: "This is so marvelous I can't believe it. I didn't think there was much hope.''

"I had no idea she wanted to contact me," Yeager said. "I figured bygones should be left as bygones and she was happy the way things were. I decided I would just let the past be gone. But I've often wondered if she was married and had children.''

She did both. Now Mrs. Jean Foster, she is a mother and a grandmother, and she has never been happier.

"I'm going to get in touch with my father," she said. "I'm very, very happy."

Sometimes I've got the greatest job in the world. This was one of those times.

Sir Walter Raleigh, alias Walter the Weasel

I Heard a Story One Time . . .

Does this sound like the kind of guy you'd like?

He was a traitor and pulled three prison terms, spending 13 years in jail.

He was firmly convinced that there was a mysterious empire in South America made of gold.

He was vain and a clothes horse.

He sold booze and was a pirate.

He organized four expeditions to unexplored territory. Two of them failed miserably and returned, but the other two disappeared — every man, woman and child.

He was given one last chance and was sent on a military mission. He stayed out of the battle that cost the life of his son and best friend, and when he came home he was executed.

One well-respected book says of him, "Sober historians, after discounting the dazzle, tend to dismiss him as a not-too-scrupulous adventurer who had little influence on events."

And he possibly was an atheist.

Surely you recognize this loser by now. He is the legendary foul-up and troublemaker we have honored by naming our capital city after him.

Yessir, that Sir Walter Raleigh was some kind of guy.

Sir Walter has been in the news lately because the city of Raleigh is looking for a new symbol. We used to use the oak tree, but a City Council member didn't like that one anymore and suggested we might use a lapel pin that looks like Sir Walter's cape, the one he was supposed to have put down for the queen to walk on.

With all of this, and the big celebration of our 400th anniversary, let's take a look at one of our founding fathers.

Walter began his slide toward failure right off the bat. First, he didn't spell his name right.

Walter spelled it "Ralegh."

He was born in 1554 in Devon, and by the time he was 15, he claimed to have been a military hero. At 23 he claimed to be a member of the queen's court, and at 24 he was a pirate robbing Spanish ships.

At 26, he participated in a battle against Irish patriots, and the Encyclopedia Britannica says he "fought with as much ruthlessness as gallantry. He was one of the officers of the day when the whole garrison of Smerwick, County Kerry, was executed."

Queen Elizabeth liked that, and at 28, Walter was a big favorite of the bald-headed queen. (Some claim he was a secret lover of the "Virgin Queen," but you know how people like to gossip. I'll stick with the facts.) She gave him a lot of stolen Irish land and a monopoly on wine licenses and broadcloth exports. She even made him a knight in 1585 when he was 31.

Then she threw him in jail when he got married without her permission. (The queen was not only bald but jealous.) He got out by paying the queen a bribe.

About this time, Walter began trying to settle America. He sent an expedition over in April 1584 to find Florida. Those explorers came back and said they couldn't find Florida but that North Carolina was a terrific place. In April 1585, Walter sent 108 men under Sir Richard Grenville, his cousin. That bunch landed on Roanoke Island Aug. 17, 1585. Grenville went back for supplies a couple of weeks later, and when he hadn't come back in 10 months the entire starving, sickly group caught a ride with Sir Francis Drake, who happened to be passing by, and headed home.

Grenville showed up a few weeks later with more people and the long-awaited groceries and persuaded all 15 men to stay behind.

Grenville left again, so Walter sent his fourth expedition, under John White, with instructions to stop at Roanoke, pick up the 15 and move the whole kit and caboodle up to Chesapeake Bay.

This fourth outfit was put ashore by sailors who refused to take them to Chesapeake. Not one of the 15 that Grenville had left was found alive.

White left these colonists behind (do you begin to see a pattern here?), and when he got back three years later they were all gone, too. There goes The Lost Colony II.

Walter went to jail for 13 years in 1603 for plotting to overthrow King James I and put the king's cousin, Arabella, on the throne. Walter obviously got along better with queens than kings.

They let him out in 1616 to go to Guiana and bring back the gold he said was there. But they told him that under no circumstances was he to fight the Spanish.

Walter got off in Trinidad and sent his friend Lawrence Keymis ahead with instructions to attack the Spanish anyway, steal the gold and hightail it back to Trinidad, after which they'd all go home heroes. Walter sent his son Walter Jr. with Keymis.

It was a disaster. Walter Jr. was killed, the expedition was thoroughly whipped, and Keymis committed suciide.

Walter made it back to England and claimed that he had missed the target by 20 miles and that he was really sorry.

He tried to run away to France, but his relatives turned him in, and on Oct. 29, 1618, he was beheaded.

Slave Girl Helped Change History

Murfreesboro
Her name was Emily Morgan, a mulatto slave girl from this Hertford County town.

Little is know about her youth or her old age, but for three days in 1836, when she was 20, she changed the course of American history and inspired one of the most popular folk songs ever written.

Emily was "The Yellow Rose of Texas" and an unwitting heroine of the battle for Texas independence.

Her story was given to me by Frank Stephenson, a faculty member at Chowan College who has written a screenplay about Emily and her exploits.

"A friend of mine named Tom Parramore, a history professor at Meredith College, came up with the original story of Emily Morgan, and I took it from there," Stephenson said. "I was amazed to find out that her story had never been told. No one knows about her, although British and Mexican journalists in Texas at the time knew of her."

The story begins in the early 1800s with James Morgan, a Murfreesboro businessman and plantation owner. Morgan had 18 or 19 slaves and was a prosperous man. The house he built, now called Myrick House, still stands on Broad Street.

Morgan went to Galveston, Texas, in 1830, drawn to the frontier by cheap land and adventure. He bought a larger ranch near Galveston and soon returned to North Carolina.

But his return home was short-lived. In 1831, a band of slaves led by Nat Turner revolted just over the state line in Virginia, less than 15 miles from the Morgan plantation and several white people were killed.

"That scared the hell out of white people around here," Stephenson said. "Morgan went down to the courthouse and changed all of his slaves to indentured servants (Mexican authorities would not allow slaves to be brought to Texas but would allow indentured servants) and left North Carolina for Texas."

One of the slaves that went with Morgan was Emily Morgan, by all reports one of the most beautiful women anyone had seen. She was of mixed racial parentage, and Stephenson says it is possible she was Morgan's daughter.

Morgan settled on his spread near Galveston at a place called Morgan's Point.

The war for Texas independence was raging by spring 1836. The Alamo had fallen to Gen. Santa Anna's Mexican forces, and the cocky general, who patterned himself after Napoleon and even carried a full-size portrait of the French leader in his tent, was heading cross country to Galveston, where he planned to put his forces on ships and sail to Mexico.

But Gen. Sam Houston had other ideas. Houston's men had been snapping at the heels of the Mexican army across the plains of Texas, but they were too small a force to meet the Mexicans in open battle.

Santa Anna's forces were burning everything they found on their march from the Alamo to the sea. He wanted to terrorize the Texans and teach them the price of rebellion.

His troops crossed Morgan's ranch at Morgan's Point, and Santa Anna give the order that every slave would be killed and the ranch burned.

But the beautiful, long-haired Emily caught his eye, and he ordered her brought to his encampment at San Jacinto.

Santa Anna was so taken by her that he ordered his men to settle in for what became a three-day furlough while he enjoyed the charms of his captive.

Those three days were all it took. His men, following the lead of their general, used the three days for a big party and were not paying attention when Houston arrived with his ragtag army of Texas volunteers.

Enraged by the slaughter at the Alamo, Houston had had enough time to assemble an army and plan a surprise attack. His men soundly whipped the Mexican army, and the defeat set the stage for Texas independence.

The battle also paved the way for the collapse of all Mexican authority in the southwest United States.

"I don't know if it was racial, the fact that a black slave girl from North Carolina did it, or if it was the sexual aspects of the story, but American history books don't record Emily Morgan," Stephenson said.

"But the earlier versions of the song 'The Yellow Rose of Texas' do identify the girl as 'Emily, the Maid of Morgan's Point.'"

Emily survived the battle of San Jacinto and returned to Morgan's ranch, Stephenson said. Nothing else was heard from her.

Bright Morning, Dark Tragedy

Sanford

It was one of those spring mornings when it feels good to go to work.

It was a snappy 43 degrees, but the sun gave promise of a perfect 72 degrees by early afternoon.

Fate had chosen a beautiful day for 54 miners to die in a black hole in the ground.

It was May 27, 1925 — the day of the Carolina Coal Co. mine disaster at the village of Coal Glen, nine miles from Sanford.

A buildup of natural gas did it, the experts said. Gas was released as the miners burrowed beneath the ground of

Chatham County. No one ever knew what spark set off the first explosion, which shook the earth at 9:40 a.m.

Mine superintendent Howard Butler was in his office when he felt the ground shake. He picked up a telephone and called to the 1,800-foot level. The explosion was deeper than that, someone thought. But then communication was lost.

Butler headed into the mine. He reached the 1,200-foot level and found a wall of rubble on top of six men, some of them still alive. A second blast rocked the mine, trapping Butler.

He scrambled over the debris and headed for the surface, clawing his way through the gas and smoke. A third blast slammed through the tortured rock just as Butler crawled out into that beautiful spring morning, sick and dazed from the gas and the horror of what he had seen.

The first rescue team into the mine made it to the 1,200-foot level. That's where they found the first six bodies. The rescuers could see that an intense fire was burning deeper in the mine, and no one had any hope that anyone would come out alive.

But miners don't leave other miners to die alone in a blackened grave. Most of these men had worked together before, down in the Alabama coal fields, and for the next three days they would do without rest to bring their friends out.

Six men at a time went into the Coal Glen mine. That's all that could work in the cramped space.

A cable tied to a coal car would tighten and begin to hum every two hours as the rescuers were brought out. A shiver would go through the crowd of 5,000 people who gathered to watch as the car appeared into the sunlight.

Six blackened men, squinting and sick from gas and terror, would stagger from the car and slowly shake their heads. By 6 p.m. the day of the blast, the first bodies had been brought out.

The widows and orphans were kept behind ropes. They stood there in silence. They knew those trapped in the mine were dead.

"We never had any hope at all from the very first," Julia Dillingham of Raleigh said of the day her husband, her father and her brother-in-law died at Coal Glen.

The best description of the families came from Ben Dixon MacNeill, The News and Observer's reporter on the scene: "They stand there quietly, numbed by the unthinkable horror that lies beneath their feet. They stare at the yawning hole down which their kin went to work this morning. They whisper together in hopeless monotones and wait. There is no hope among them anywhere.

"Aged mothers stare with dry eyes, and little children tug at their skirts. Beyond them eddies a vast assemblage of people who come hundreds of miles to see a tragedy, but there is no tragedy to see, just a hole in the ground."

Sixteen bodies had been removed by the second day, but the going was slower now. The rubble had to be hauled to the surface because the side passages were full. The rescuers were at 1,700 feet. They could see a pile of bodies beyond the rubble in front of them. It looked like the miners had rushed into the main corridor at the first blast only to be killed by the second as they headed for the surface.

The bodies were severely burned and broken by the explosion and fire. Most of the victims had died instantly — the only good news the families ever heard.

The work went on around the clock. Men would argue with each other for the right to go back into that hellish hole in the ground, the right to do what they could for the miners that could have just as easily been them.

The dead were laid out under a tent so the families could come and identify them. Relatives filed past each time a new group of bodies was brought to the surface.

By the end of the third day, a Friday, 48 bodies were on the surface and four more had been found but not uncovered. It would take 10 days to bring the last body out.

Funerals and burials already had begun at a churchyard a half mile away. The haste was necesssary because of the condition of the bodies.

Late on the third day, MacNeill walked down the only street in the company town where the miners lived. He wrote: "The village street is quiet under a leaden sky. Late afternoon and many of the widows and the children, the mothers and the fathers of those who are gone have fallen asleep.

"Sleep will heal their wounds to the point where the stricken can weep. Intermittently there have been hysterical wails coming up through the gloom, but few faces have been wet by healing tears.

"Their eyes are hard, dry and lifeless."

It's Time to Remember Wiley Sauls

Henry Wyatt probably deserves having his statue on Capitol Square in Raleigh.

Most people would be hard pressed to tell you who Henry

Wyatt is, but that is nothing unusual. There are several people memorialized on the grounds that are even more obscure to the average person in North Carolina.

What Henry Wyatt did was die. He is said to be the first Confederate soldier to die in battle in the Civil War.

He was a 20-year-old soldier from Egecombe County. On June 10, 1861, Henry Wyatt and four other soldiers climbed over the breastworks at Bethel Church in Virginia, and the young North Carolina lad took a musket ball between the eyes. He died instantly.

But what do we do to remember Wiley Sauls? Where is his statue? How do we pay homage to the first North Carolinian to shed his blood for the glorious cause?

The date was May 20, 1861, the day that North Carolina seceded from the United States of America. North Carolina was the last Southern state to join the Confederacy, and as you can imagine, May 20 was quite a day in the staid old capital.

Crowds had gathered around the square to await the vote by the Legislature. The plan was to have a battery of artillery fire a salute to the Confederacy at the exact moment that North Carolina joined.

The big guns were drawn up on the west side of the square looking down Hillsborough Street. The crowd was rowdy and full of Southern pride, among other things, and a military band kept spirits high with sprightly tunes.

Precisely at noon the signal came. A white handkerchief was waved from a Capitol window and, at the same moment, the U.S. flag began to come down. As the Confederate flag was being raised, the artillerymen let loose with a mighty volley in salute.

Wiley Sauls of Wake County was one of those artillerymen. His job was to take a long ramrod and swab the cannon barrels before the next round was fired.

Right in mid-swab, Wiley dropped his ramrod, stood on his tiptoes, lurched forward and grabbed his behind.

Wiley spun around, and the entire crowd witnessed the shedding of his Southern blood.

A very large, very angry bulldog had latched on to Sauls, right in the portion of his anatomy where one would least like a bulldog to afix itself.

Witnesses later said that in the heat of the moment, it being secession day and all, Wiley accidentally had whacked the bulldog between the eyes with his ramrod.

It took a moment for the bulldog to regain his composure, and when he did, Sauls, leaning forward, presented a target of opportunity too good to be ignored.

Wiley did what he could, which wasn't much. He twisted, turned and danced about, which did no good because the bulldog was equipped with splendid jaws.

History does not record how Wiley and the dog came to a parting of the ways, but history recalls that later, in a parade down Hillsborough Street, Wiley was seen leaning forward over a caisson, his aft portion raised and covered with a bloody cloth sack.

I am pleased to report that Wiley recovered from his historic injury, served with valor throughout the rest of the war and came home without another scratch.

No, dear readers, I didn't make it up. This little drama was recorded for posterity by Joseph Lacy Seawell, for 38 years an office boy, deputy clerk and clerk of the N.C. Supreme Court.

The incident had one other historic element. It also led to the shaving of one Shad Moss, who supposedly had not scraped his beard in 20 years.

It seems that Shad owned the bulldog in question, and Wiley once he recovered, went in search of the offending pup.

The two had a discussion about the advisability of sending the bulldog to Doggy Heaven. I'm sure you can understand Wiley's position. Wiley's hands became entangled in Shad's long red beard and when they finally separated, a goodly portion of the whiskers were missing. Shad's wife said it looked "so scarified" that Shad shaved.

Fame for One of the Bad Guys

Carbonton

History often is stories about people so goody-goody they make you ill.

You go through those old homes, and they tell you how wonderful all those dead people were.

I don't know about you, but every now and then I crave a real jerk, a guy who turned out so bad the doctor should have slapped his mama when he was born.

Meet the infamous Phillip Alston, the builder and master of The House in the Horseshoe, a state historic site in Moore County.

Alston was from Halifax, back when it was the center of civilization for much of North Carolina. No one knows when he took off for the high ground on the banks of the Deep River, but they know why.

"He was charged with counterfeiting," said Royal Windley, site manager of the restored House in the Horseshoe.

"I tell people he was a wealthy man. He should have been because he made his own money. He was really not a very nice man."

To make sure no one would like him, Alston also went around telling people he was an atheist. You can imagine how popular an atheist counterfeiter was in those days.

Alston settled on 4,000 acres in a horseshoe bend in the river, a sizable spread even then. But he had some ideas about how to get even more land.

When the Revolutionary War broke out, Alston became a rebel leader.

He was a justice of the peace, and his job was to go around making Scottish farmers sign a pledge of allegiance to the United States. If he came across a piece of land he liked, he would not let the owner sign the pledge even when the owner begged to sign. Alston would ship him off to a camp in Pennsylvania where they sent people they didn't trust.

Alston then would steal the land. He soon had 7,000 acres.

David Fanning from Johnston County was just about as mean, ruthless and unpopular as Alston. The difference was that Fanning fought for the British.

Fanning heard what Alston was doing to the Scots, many of whom had sided with the king, so he took a band of Loyalists and headed up-country to take out Alston.

One day, Alston and his band of men were coming through what is now Southern Pines when they came across Kenneth Black, one of Fanning's men. Black was leading Fanning's lame bay horse while Fanning rode to Cross Creek with a group of prisoners.

Alston took Black's gun, whipped Black and left him to die.

Fanning came back, and Black, with his dying breath, fingered Alston as the man who had beaten him.

Fanning went after Alston with a vengeance.

He found Alston at dawn on Sunday, Aug. 5, 1781.

Alston was in his house. His men were sleeping outside. Fanning and his troops crept up to the house and opened fire.

The battle raged for a couple of hours until Fanning, fearing that other rebels would arrive and cut him off, pulled up a wagon full of hay and set it on fire.

Then he started pushing it toward the house, planning to burn up the whole lot of them.

That was enough for Alston's wife, Temperance. She had hidden the children in the chimney so they wouldn't get shot, but revolution or no revolution, she was not about to be burned to death.

She grabbed a white bedsheet and ran out on the porch, figuring a guy like Fanning probably would shoot a man who tried to surrender but wouldn't shoot a woman.

She was right. The firing stopped. Alston and Fanning met on the front porch. Alston surrendered himself and his men and promised not to fight any more. Of course, the war was almost over, so it didn't matter.

Alston went on to great fame in politics. He was clerk of court at one time and was elected to the state Senate.

He worked out a deal for a man named George Glascock to serve as clerk of court until Alston's son was old enough to take the job. Glascock was then to step down.

But Glascock liked the job and decided to keep it.

So Alston had him shot.

What he did was throw a huge party at the house, and while everyone was having a big time and he had an alibi, he sent his slave, Dave, to Glascock's house (Glascock was not invited) to shoot him.

Dave did it and got caught. Alston put up bail for Dave, and Dave took off for parts unknown.

Everyone knew what had happened, and Alston was charged with murder because the law said that if a slave committed a crime and could not be punished, the owner had to pay the penalty.

Alston, faced with murder, took off for Georgia.

There, on Oct. 28, 1791, while he slept in bed, someone fired a shot through his window and killed Alston. Some say Dave did it because Alston hadn't protected him. No matter who it was, nobody mourned him much.

Rx: Always Wear Clothes

It happened across the border in Darlington, S.C., during a fierce cold spell.

A Darlington optometrist named Hobbs was taking a long, hot, relaxing bath one night when he heard his burglar alarm. He knew something was wrong because the alarm was not supposed to be turned on, much less go off.

He also realized the burglar alarm was wired to call the police and the fire department when it went off, so he had to do something quick. The first thing he could figure out was that the house must be on fire and that the fire somehow had tripped the alarm.

Bounding out of the warm tub wearing only a worried frown and a few soap bubbles, Hobbs tore upstairs to find the fire.

There was no fire. What he found instead was a broken water line and water gushing all over the place. I don't know about you, but broken water lines can make a man panic.

He immediately thought to cut off the water coming into the house. Good move. He did not, however, immediately think to get dressed first. Bad move.

He flew down the steps and out into his back yard looking for the water cutoff. Perhaps he should have stopped first to look for his pants, but it was a bit of an emergency and it was dark. So he gave it a shot.

Had he found the cutoff valve and made it back into the house safely, he would have had but a brief anecdote to tell friends. But that didn't happen.

"It was about 8 p.m., and I was squatting in the bushes looking for the valve," Dr. Hobbs told his hometown newspaper. "I was nude, and the next thing I knew a flashlight turned on about 10 feet away. A gruff voice said, 'Put your hands on your head and stand up slowly.' "

The burglar alarm was on the job. It had called the police department, which had responded in a flash.

Still squatting, the doctor told the officer that, he was buck naked and besides, he lived in the house.

"The voice got even firmer," Dr. Hobbs said. "He said, 'Put your hands on your head and stand up slowly.'

" 'Hey man, you've got to be kidding,' I replied. 'I'm naked.' "

No, the policeman was not kidding. Look at it this way. If you were sent to investigate a burglar alarm at a doctor's house and found a naked man hidding in the bushes in the back yard, would you be kidding?

What finally convinced the doctor to stand as ordered was a sound that gets anyone's attention, the sound of a policeman's gun being cocked to fire. It is one of those sounds you only have to hear once to immediately recognize.

The frozen and naked doctor stood rigidly at attention and was ordered to march out of the bushes and into the driveway.

"The policeman started questioning me," Hobbs said. "I put my hands down and he ordered me to put them up again."

Hobbs tried to reason, between shivers, with the officer. He tried to point out that it would be rather foolish for someone to break into a house on a night when it was 10 degrees while wearing nothing but what he came to this world wearing.

The policeman, however, was well aware that people often do bizarre and unexplainable things and that this seemed like another one of those times — a good story for the boys down at the station house but not so funny that he was going to drop his weapon. It was pretty obvious, though, that the doctor did not have a concealed weapon on him. I mean, where would it have been concealed?

Hobbs kept trying to convince the police officer that he was an upstanding member of the medical profession who happened to be cavorting naked at night in the midst of a hard freeze. Finally, he convinced the officer to go inside with him and see for himself. It could have been the icicle on his nose that did it.

Once they got inside, Hobbs showed the officer the broken water pipe and got dressed and then, wouldn't you know it, the officer started laughing and saying how the fellows down at the station were not going to believe this one. I am sure Dr. Hobbs shared his merriment.

But not right then. It takes a little while to see how funny it is to be arrested buck naked in your backyard when it is 10 degrees and water is pouring into your house.

"I can tell you one thing for certain," the doctor said. "It was the first time I ever had a gun pointed at me. Whether you are dressed or undressed, it makes you think when you are staring down the barrel of a revolver."

It's a Hair-Raising Tale

I love a good tale whether it is true or not.

This story sent to me by Ruby Perry of Sharpsburg fits that category:

Seems that a fellow was working in his garage when he caught the seat of his pants on a nail.

He tugged, the nail held, and the pocket on the back of the man's pants was ripped slam off.

The man's wife, apparently not being one who wanted to cut out and sew on a new pocket — but then who would? — got one of those store-bought pockets and put it on as a replacement.

But there was a problem with the new, store-bought pocket. It was way too narrow and way too deep.

Now most of us menfolks keep our wallets in the same pocket on the same side all the time, so the man was determined that the new pocket was where he would put his wallet.

He pushed, shoved, jammed and crammed, and finally the bulging wallet had a new home, even though it was a tight fit.

Then the fellow, exhausted by his labors and a big supper, settled back in his favorite recliner for an early evening nap.

He awoke refreshed and decided to take a stroll around the neighborhood even though it was getting on toward dark. There was nothing on television worth watching anyway.

He had gone but a short distance from his house when out of the bushes leaped a burly thug with a gun in his hand. The thug jammed the gun into the belly of the man and demanded his money.

The man knew that the wallet contained little but a few credit cards, some pictures, the stuff that men like to stick in wallets to show to one another down at the service station — but not very much money.

He told the thug that the wallet was in his left rear pocket.

"Get it out," said the thug.

The man reached around and tried to do as the thug demanded, but the wallet was stuck in the too-narrow and too-deep, store-bought pocket.

He tried with his left hand, and that didn't work. He tried to twist around with his right hand, and that didn't work as well as the left hand. Mostly, he looked like a dog trying to chase its tail. He couldn't even get his hand in the pocket, much less get the wallet out.

"Quit stalling," said the thug.

"You try," said the frightened man, whereupon he turned around and raised his hands again so the thug would not shoot him.

The thug tugged and tugged. He tugged so hard he lifted the man slam off the ground, leaving him dancing on tiptoe and hoping the thug wouldn't pull much higher because it might start hurting in another inch or so.

The wallet, snug in the too-narrow and too-deep, store-bought pocket, did not budge — even with the thug's tug.

"Take your pants off," said the thug, now tired of tugging.

"Sure enough," said the man and dropped his pants down around his ankles.

It was then he realized that his work shoes were much bigger than the pants' legs and the pants were not going to come off unless he removed his shoes.

"Take off your shoes," said the thug. He was getting a bit tired of all this. A 10-second mugging was turning into a comic opera.

"Sure enough," said the man as he sat on the ground to untie his shoes. It was then he discovered that someone — could it have been his darling grandson? — had tied his shoe laces into a hard knot while he was sleeping the sleep of the just in his recliner.

Just about that moment, a car came around the corner. The burly mugging thug grabbed the man by the hair on his head, planning to drag him into the bushes out of sight.

But, as you might have figured out by this time, that didn't work either.

The thug grabbed a handful of hair, yanked pretty hard and ended up with a real nice toupee in his hand.

Wouldn't you know it, in the car was the law.

The thug dropped the toupee, figuring he'd scalped the poor man, dropped the gun in surprise and fled back into the bushes. The man grabbed both the gun and the toupee as the thug dug out.

Now not all policemen are ace detectives, but these constables could tell there was something wrong when they saw a bald-headed man with his pants down around his ankles holding a headful of hair in one hand and a gun in the other.

They were standing there with their spotlight on the poor man and their guns drawn when out of the bushes came the thug at a dead run, with a large dog latched onto his own seat.

He will probably need a new pocket on his pants, too.

The original version of that story was written by Cleve Wilkie for the Baptist State Convention of North Carolina, and Ruby said she saw it in The Franklin Times.

Thanks to Cleve and Ruby for a good story.

The Horselaugh Was on a Mule

I never met Edmund Hoyt Harding, but like thousands of lucky North Carolinians, I got to hear him speak one time.

Harding was from Washington, N.C., and he was the greatest storyteller I ever heard. I don't remember the occasion, but I remember it was in a warehouse, an appropriate place for the former fertilizer salesman turned professional humorist to reduce a crowd to tears of laughter.

Harding died in September 1970, and this was his funniest story.

I remembered the bare bones of the tale, but it was R. L. Shearin of Cary who filled in the missing details.

Get another cup of coffee and sit back and enjoy the tale of Horace the Mule.

A country lady of the Albermarle region had a mule named Horace. Horace was taken sick one day, and the distraught lady called the veterinarian and asked him to take a look at her good mule.

It was getting on late in the day, and in those days, it could take a while to get anywhere. The overworked vet was more interested in supper than mules at that late hour, so he told the lady to give Horace a sizable dose of mineral oil to get him through the night and if he wasn't better by daylight to give him another call and he'd go out and check on him.

Knowing full well that a sick mule can be somewhat cantankerous, the good woman asked the doctor just how she was supposed to go about giving Horace the medicine without getting bitten.

The doctor told her to use a funnel, and just to make sure that Horace did not bite her, the doctor suggested she give him the mineral oil through the end with which anyone who ever has done much plowing is most familiar.

Poor Horace was awful sickly, and when the lady went out to the barn, there stood Horace, just a pitiful-looking thing with his head hanging low and the occasional moan escaping his floppy lips.

The lady looked for a funnel, but there wasn't one around. But there, hanging on the barn wall, was a beautiful fox horn. This was a wonderful fox horn. It was gold-plated and had red tassels. It was truly a sight to see.

So the lady took down the gold-plated, red-tasseled fox horn and put it where the doctor ordered. Horace didn't bat an eye.

The lady then reached up on a high shelf for the medicine, but instead of grabbing the mineral oil, the concerned and somewhat nervous — and some might even say slightly abashed — lady picked up a bottle of turpentine.

She gave Horace a sizable slug via the gold-plated, red-tasseled fox horn.

You could say this surprised Horace.

He let out a mightly bellow that they say you could have heard for a country mile, and that is a long way. He bucked; he kicked; he generally tore up the place. The lady screamed and ran, and Horace kicked out the barn wall. The lady grabbed the ladder and headed for the hayloft, and Horace headed over the nearest fence.

He went down the dirt road just a-raising cain and kicking up his heels every few feet. Every time he kicked, the fox horn would blow.

Now any good foxhound knows that when the fox horn sounds, it is time to hunt, and a foxhound surely loves to hunt, so every hound in the neighborhood fell in behind Horace.

There they went, Horace kicking, the fox horn sounding its mournful call, the gold-plated horn gleaming in the setting sun, the red tassels waving in the breeze and the happy hounds barking at full throat.

The strange parade happened to go by the home of Old Man Buffkin. Now Old Man Buffkin had been known to take a drink or two in his time, like every hour or so for the past 15 years since his wife ran off with the lightning rod salesman, and he was somewhat amazed at the sight that unfolded in front of his bleary eyes. They say he got up and broke every liquor bottle in the house and never took even a Christmas nip everafter.

It was getting well on toward dark by that time, and Horace and the hounds were nearing the Intracostal Waterway.

The bridge tender on duty heard the horn blowing and assumed it was a boat needing to cross through the bridge.

He went out and opened the bridge as the horn got louder and louder.

Horace hit the open bridge and went head first into the water, followed closely by the baying hounds.

The hounds swam out to safety, but Horace didn't make it. There were a couple of bubbles and that was it.

Now it happens that the bridge tender was a country politician and was running for county sheriff, but he lost the election in a landslide. In fact, Old Man Buffkin was the only person who voted for him.

The rest of the voters figured that a man who didn't know the difference between a mule with a horn up his rear and a boat on the water didn't have any business being sheriff.

Old Ex-Rebel Gets the Last Yell

I ran across this one in Greenville, S.C. They've got a columnist there named Reese Fant and this story is his. I'm going to steal it before someone else does. It is too good to be true . . . and too good not to pass along.

The setting is Anderson, S.C., shortly after the War of Northern Aggression. Our brave boys in gray lost that one and therefore had to put up with the indignity of Yankee occupation.

South Carolinians really got it in the neck because they started the whole thing.

Both sides were still pretty much sore about the whole business right after the war and the commander of the Yankee troops stationed in Anderson liked to pick on the Southerners, so every morning he'd march his blueclads up to the town square where they'd do a little drilling.

There was an old Rebel sitting on the front porch of the town's hotel. He used to watch the uppity Yanks drilling there on holy ground, and one day it got the best of him.

He waited until things got real quiet and then he yelled out, "You Yankees won the war, but us rebels whupped the hell out of you at Chickamauga."

That really made the Yankees hot, mostly because the old man was right. The Rebels had whupped the Yankees at Chickamauga.

The Yankee captain took it that first day and didn't say a thing. But the old man was back the next day.

"You Yankees won the war, but us Rebels whupped the hell out of you at Chickamauga."

And he was back every day, yelling the same thing.

Finally the Yankee captain had enough. He lined up his soldiers nice and neat and they all marched over to where the old Rebel sat on the hotel porch. He was ordered to step down off the porch. Then they arrested him.

The captain told the old soldier that he would have to stay in jail until he signed a loyalty oath to the Yankee government and promised to stop saying such things.

The old Rebel thought about that for a moment, then said that he would rot in jail before he'd sign such a blasphemous thing.

The captain took the old boy off to jail.

The old soldier held out for seven days and then he said he'd sign their blamed loyalty oath.

He did, and they let him go.

The next morning the Yankees marched into the square for their morning drill, and there sat the old Rebel on the hotel porch, right where he'd always been.

They marched around and waited to see what the old man would do.

He didn't say a word. He just sat there, staring at the Yankees.

That went on for several days. The Yankees watched him, and

he watched the Yankees. Silence. The Yankees figured their troubles were over. The old rebel had learned his lesson.

Finally, as they say down home, the devil flew in the old man and he could stand it no longer.

The troops were lined up nice and neat when across the little town square came an authentic Rebel Yell.

The troops looked at the old man, remembering the loyalty oath he had taken and knowing he'd go back to jail if he said the first thing wrong.

He waited until he had their attention and in his strongest voice yelled:

"Us Yankees won the war, but those Rebels whupped the hell out of us at Chickamauga."

The Funny Side of World War II

I just love this letter from Nancye Lindsey of Raleigh:

"I watched the three-hour special about President Franklin D. Roosevelt with mixed feelings since I was a brat in that era. I was too young to appreciate the Depression, but I came into World War II as a boy-crazy teenager.

"War is hell, yet most everything has a funny side and that war was no exception.

"For instance, the Sacrifice for Victory Committee took away all our elastic. What did they do with it? Retread tires? Use it for red tape?

"Beats me. All I know is that female underpants were without the stuff and were held together with one lone, flimsy, precarious button.

"Can you just imagine trying to abandon yourself to a wild jitterbug with the thought lurking in the back of your mind that one small convolution of the body could reveal your taste in lingerie to a vast audience?

"I saw one poor girl's worst fears realized and she danged near invented a new step when 'they' fell to her ankles.

"Now I can personally tell your about garter belts. They didn't have no stretch neither.

"I had a hot dinner date after work. At 4:57 p.m. (I was a clock watcher), the hook on mine tore away from the fabric. I borrowed a safety pin from a co-worker (the worst decision I ever made) and it wasn't safe at all.

"I was sashaying right up Fayetteville Street toward the California Restaurant on the arm of my meal ticket when it parted company.

"As the whole contraption descended it only encountered mild resistance from the cowardly button on those 'other things.'

"Thank the Lord for lightning reflexes. My knees came together like a pair of castanets and my date was either too shy or too courteous to ask me why I was suddenly pigeon-toed.

"I made it to the restroom and shed the whole shebang, but that turkey never asked me out again. Men. Bah!

"Ah, but we had good times, too. There were those USO dances at Fort Bragg when we gussied up, pinned a flower in our hair, rode the bus through Fuquay and Varina — separate towns then — and Lillington, picking up more eager girls on the way to 'where the boys are.'

"At the Main Post Club, females lined up at one end and males at the other to come together for the first dance. My best friend and I were both extremely nearsighted and couldn't see two feet ahead without help, but glasses were neither chic nor cool then so we always left our glasses on the bus.

"As a result, the other girls could see who they were going to be paired with and could shift around in the line until they got a good-looking guy. We were left with whatever was leftover.

"Fortunately, all Fred Astaires don't look like Clark Gable so we probably got the best dancers through poor eyesight. Besides, when you're talking about 75 girls and 200 boys, there is no such thing as a wallflower.

"Most everybody I knew worked for 'The Cause'; I got a job with the ODT (Office of Defense Transportation, you know). I think they mainly rationed gas to trucks but I wouldn't swear to it.

"I was given a desk complete with telephone and told to call all the garages in town and try to locate critical parts for trucks all over the South. I didn't know a crankshaft from a hole in the ground, but thank goodness the Japanese didn't know that or we'd have lost the war for sure. As it was, every now and then I'd find one of those strange parts and feel like I'd discovered America all over again.

"There is more nostalgia of a time when we all proudly waved the flag, remembered the taste of butter while loving the idea of GIs getting it, savored that rationed coffee, cheered the victories and wept over the defeats and all pulled together.

"Will we ever know that special feeling again? Probably not.

"Thanks for letting me live that part of my life again. You write so often about the sad reminiscences of those years that I think you should know there were humorous and poignant aspects, too.

"The Roosevelt years were special to so many of us who lived through them and truly enjoyed togetherness as we never will again.

"God bless America, pantyhose and butter."

The Great Bull Calf Walk

I can't help but wish Kerr Scott were still governor.

Don't get me wrong. The current crop of politicians is probably all right, but they have been sanitized, packaged and programmed until the last ounce of juice has been squeezed right out of them.

But Kerr Scott, the branchhead boy from Haw River, the rabbit huntin', tobacco chewin', chitlin eatin' governor from 1949 to 1953 and hardly a media adviser's dream child, was a different sort of fellow. The man had Country Style.

They still tell stories in Eastern North Carolina about the greatest campaign stunt ever pulled in these parts, the legendary Kerr Scott Great Bull Calf Walk.

"Nobody ever expected it to turn out like it did," said Tom Davis of Pink HIll. "I was the co-chairman of the thing, and it about ran me crazy."

The year was 1954. Scott had left the governor's office and was running for the Democratic nomination for U.S. senator, and in those days, winning the Democratic primary was tantamount to winning the whole shebang.

The official version is that Scott went on a radio program in Kinston hosted by Alice Aycock and told a story — who knows whether it was true or not? — about how back in 1919 he had walked from Kinston to Hargett's Store, a distance of 21 miles, in six hours.

Scott said a taxi driver had offered to take him for a dollar a mile, but "I'd walked many a mile for nothing, so I could walk 21 miles for a dollar a mile."

Not content to leave it at that, Scott bragged that no one could walk it faster than he had, and furthermore, if anyone did, he'd give them a bull calf.

A few months later, The Great Bull Calf Walk was held, and 39 purebred Jersey bulls were handed out.

"It was amazing," Davis said. "Forty people walked, and all but one of them did it in less than six hours."

But it wasn't as spontaneous as Scott pretended.

"Kerr told us the night before he went on the radio that he was thinking about doing it, and we all urged him to go ahead," said Davis, who was Scott's area campaign manager.

"We expected maybe a half-dozen people would show up, and we'd get a little publicity. We had to stop when it got to 40 people. That's a lot of bull calves."

But the bet was on, and as Davis said, "When Kerr Scott told you he'd do something, you could take it to the bank, so we had to do it."

Registration for the great event was closed within days of the dare.

Late on the afternoon of March 3, 1954, 40 walkers took off from Kinston headed for Hargett's Store. An estimated 1,500 to 2,000 cars and trucks lined the route to watch them on their trek. Newspaper people from all over the state had gathered. Life magazine would write about it. There was a massive traffic jam.

Hardrock Simpson led the pack. The postman from Burlington was a famous walker of the day. The story goes that one time Hardrock outwalked a horse across the United States. He made it, but the horse died. Or so the story goes.

Hardrock crossed the finish line in four hours and eight minutes. Thirty-eight others trudged in within six hours.

"Then we had to find 39 bull calves," Davis said. "We got them from everywhere, and every one of them was donated. It didn't cost the campaign a dime. Some of them even came from South Carolina. Kerr Scott had a lot of friends in the dairy business. As it turned out, he didn't even have to give one of his own."

On May 1, the great giveaway was staged in Pink Hill. All of the winners were there, and all of the calves were there. Kerr Scott and his beloved Miss Mary rode through the town of 400 on a sulky pulled by a gray mule, and 5,000 people were there to watch.

Membership cards in the Athletic Order of the Survivors of the Great Bull Calf Walk were passed out to all who walked or helped, and when Hardrock Simpson stepped up to claim his prize, the calf stomped on Scott's foot. It was perfect public relations.

"We gave away a lot of calves that day," Davis said, "and to tell the truth, some of the folks who got one didn't deserve it.

They caught rides to make it, but we didn't say anything. The publicity was worth it."

It would be Scott's last campaign. He won his Senate seat and died in office.

"There won't ever be another one like Kerr Scott," Davis said.

Mother Nature Shows Compassion

Topsail Beach

Mary Lou and Louis Muery traveled the world for 32 years as a Navy family before they settled on this narrow barrier island 12 years ago.

The fascination that brought them to this place by the sea has not ebbed.

"I have the privilege of living on an island like this and seeing extraordinary things every day," Mary Lou says.

But no sight ever will be more extraordinary than what Louis and Mary Lou saw at dawn on the morning of Jan. 31, 1981.

They were exhausted when they went to bed in their seaside home the night before. Mary Lou runs a popular gift shop at Topsail Beach, and they traditionally spend each January traveling and buying merchandise for the next season. They came home on the last day of the month and fell into bed.

The first eerie sound came in the darkness just before dawn.

"I can only describe it as the sound of a human being in agony," Mary Lou said. "I immediately thought someone was in distress."

Mary Lou got up and went to the bedroom window that overlooks the beach. She threw open the drapes and looked out into the predawn. She saw nothing; nor did Louis, who was in another part of the house doing his morning exercises with a jump rope.

"I thought I must have heard it in a dream," she said. "I know we were weary from the trip, and I thought I must have had a nightmare."

She went back to bed, and about two minutes later, as she lay there trying to go back to sleep, she heard it again. Again, it sounded like the cry of a human in torment, a high, moaning, wailing sound that chilled her.

She called Louis from his exercise, and the two of them went out onto the deck and looked toward the sea.

"You know how dawn is — one minute you can't see anything and the next minute you can," she said. "Well, this time I could see more.

"When you live on the beach, the ocean is a familiar scene. You notice when something is awry, and I immediately knew something was different out there."

Before them, perhaps 40 feet from the edge of the ocean, in a slough between the beach and an off-shore sandbar, were more porpoises than either of them had ever seen.

Mary Lou says there were well over 100 porpoises. Louis says there were that many just on the surface, and no one knows how many were underneath the water.

It was a turbulent, swirling school of large porpoises and they seemed to be doing something, but what?

"Again, we heard that cry," Mary Lou said. "I could feel it through my entire body."

Then they saw it.

There in the slough, surrounded by an uncountable school of leaping, splashing porpoises, was a baby whale about 15 feet long.

He was trapped in the shallow water, unable to cross the sandbar to the deep water where — just at that moment — Mary Lou and Louis saw what was making that plaintive, mournful cry.

It was a female whale, perhaps 50 feet long or longer. Her baby was trapped between the sandbar and the beach, and she was in agony.

They could see her and hear her cry. They could see the baby and watch it thrash, and they could see the porpoises. The mother whale made one last cry and dove beneath the waves, her giant tail tossing in the air.

And then it happened — one of those things in nature that no one can explain.

The huge school of porpoises surrounded the baby whale, and somehow they got it back over the sandbar to the deeper water where its frantic mother waited.

Did they gently push and shove the baby to a cut in the bar where he could swim through to open water?

Or did they somehow get beneath the baby and boost him over the bar?

Whatever the porpoises did, they did it together, working as a team to come to the aid of another creature.

The mother and the baby were reunited out to sea and safety.

"I was overwhelmed by it," Mary Lou said. "I still get tears in my eyes when I think of it.'"

A Story of Racing and the Devil

Bath

Heber Latham, 66, is a no-nonsense kind of man, a soft-spoken native of these low-lying lands.

"I don't believe in witchcraft or superstition or mess like that," he said. "But right there are those holes in the ground for you to see.

"I don't know how you account for them, but there they are.

"They have been there all my life, and there's been no change in them that I can see."

Collectors of folklore and legend call them the "Devil's Hoofprints." They have been a local legend for — depending on whom you listen to — 130-150 years.

They are small holes in the ground that have remained in the same place all that time. Latham's grandmother died at the age of 82 in 1949, and she told Latham that she had seen them all her life and they hadn't changed.

The holes are 4 to 5 inches deep with sloping sides of about 6 to 10 inches, but there the rational must give way to the irrational.

The legend is told and retold that once — some say on Sunday, Oct. 13, 1813 — a man named Elliott raced the devil and lost.

Elliott, the story goes, was a famed horseman and was getting ready for a big race the next day in Bath. A profane man, Elliott began drinking that Sunday morning and, about the time church was letting out, was riding up a country lane when he met a mysterious stranger on a beautiful horse.

The two began talking as they rode toward Bath, where Elliott was going to practice for the race. They told each other they were brilliant horsemen and both said they expected to win.

The argument grew hotter as they rode, and soon the mysterious stranger — some say his name was Buckingame — challenged Elliott to settle the matter right then.

People coming home that day from church heard the drunken Elliott say, "I'll ride this horse to victory or I'll ride this horse to hell." They heard the stranger give a soft laugh.

With that, the two horses leaped forward, pounding along the narrow country lane.

They were side by side at full speed, two magnificent stallions. Suddenly, Elliott's horse screamed in terror, turned to the right and plunged into the woods.

Elliott was thrown against a tree and killed instantly, as was his beautiful horse. The tree, legend has it, also died.

The mysterious stranger disappeared and never was seen again. His hoofprints simply stopped in the middle of the road.

To this day, the hoofprints of Elliott's charging horse are there in the thicket.

That is the legend.

The fact is, there are holes in the ground that have remained unchanged. Once, a man named Edward Cutler, who owned the land, had a hog pen there.

"The hogs would not eat the corn that fell into those holes," said Sarah Cutler, whose husband was Cutler's grandson and who now owns the land. "And after they got rid of the hog pen, the hoofprints came back, right where they had been."

It is said that an item placed in the hoofprints is gone the next day. I don't know. I do know that the hoofprints are surrounded by a thick carpet of fallen pine straw.

But the holes are remarkably free of pine straw and limbs. There were three or four pieces of pine straw in one of them, it could have fallen within the hour, but they stand out in stark relief against the brown carpet around them.

The other hoofprints were completely clear. There is no reason for that. Pine straw falls where it will, but it didn't fall in those hoofprints.

The site has been visited by thousands of people. They have driven stakes into the prints, logging trucks have run over them, people have covered them with dirt, hogs have trampled them into a muddy slush, but they are still there, unchanged after all these years.

I feel a little foolish even telling you about them. I went prepared to debunk the legend. I didn't see the Marco Light, I didn't see anything odd about the Devil's Tramping Ground. I don't believe in things like this.

But those holes are there. I don't understand it. I cannot explain it.

"The only explanation that seems to fit is that the legend is true," Latham said. "Nothing else explains it."

Friends and Neighbors

There is a cold, empty feeling when your baby does you wrong, when there is nothing left to do but button up your heart and walk way.

It feels like a winter day: gray, damp and lonely.

Danny Joe Reagan sings a song about leaving old love behind that goes: "Now you've got the nerve to ask me where I'm going, but I don't think I'd tell you if I knew. And it sure smells like snow in Bossier City."

He's a sad poet with dark blond hair hanging to his shoulders, a cowboy hat shading his closed eyes. He hunches over the microphone and rips those sad songs from his blues singer's heart. His face is battered but childlike in its vulnerability. He hurts easily.

Some nights it works. Some nights the cowboys and the kickers, the fast talkers and the slow dancers take it all in, and they share the pain that shows in Reagan's face. They grow quiet and drink another beer as they remember.

This night is not one of those. These are mostly college kids, and it is ladies' night at a honky-tonk — free admission and nickel beer for the cowgirls. They've come to party to the Bill Lyerly Band, and Danny Joe Reagan is only the warm-up act. There still is time to get another beer and do some semi-serious cruising before the party starts rocking.

They don't want to think about broken hearts. Not yet, not while the night is young and there is time to hope.

But some do pay attention. Most of those are older and wiser, and they sit back in the shadows. They know what Danny Joe Reagan is all about. Their applause smatters over the hubbub of the mating ritual swirling around them.

"It is wonderful when it works, when there is communication," Reagan said. "But even when there isn't, you know you've got some fans out there who believe in you and know what you're doing. They keep you going."

It is not easy to be this 33-year-old country singer. He is good, and his friends hope he knows it. He's been told it by Waylon Jennings, with whom he worked for a year. He's been told it by Willie Nelson, who said to keep singing, that one day his music would be accepted. He's been told it by every country music singer and musician with whom he has worked.

Bill Lyerly says, "Danny Joe Reagan is the greatest undiscovered country singer in the world."

Clyde Mattocks, leader of the Super Grit Cowboy Band, says, "Danny Joe Reagan is my favorite singer."

Tommy Worthington, owner of the Carolina Opry House, says, "Danny Joe Reagan, ain't he something?"

All he does is break my heart every time I hear him.

His life reads like the songs he sings. His mother gave him a guitar on his 14th birthday and then died a few months later, leaving him with two younger brothers to raise by himself in a farm house up a dirt path near Holy Springs.

"I never had any kind of relationship with my Daddy," he said. "After Mom died, he wasn't around much any more. I've seen the time when I had to give my little brothers popcorn for breakfast because that was all we had to eat."

But the music was there, music his mama taught him before she died, music he used to hear on the radio late at night, the music of George Jones, Merle Haggard and Hank Williams.

There were a lot of bands along the way. He played in military clubs while he was a soldier in Vietnam; he played with rock and beach music bands; he played anything, every chance he got.

He was there when they formed the Tumbleweed Band, one of the early bands that helped bring live country music back to North Carolina.

But after six years with Tumbleweed, he went out on his own, trying to play his music the way he heard it in his heart.

Waylon Jennings heard him play and hired him on the spot to be part of his traveling show. That lasted for a year until Waylon got too rich and too tired to stay on the road, and Danny was left on his own again.

"I've survived because of friends," Reagan said. "I never got married because I could never love a woman as much as I love the music, and it wouldn't be fair for a woman to be in second place.

"Friends have given me a place to stay and food to eat and, yeah, that hurts me a lot, probably more than it ought to, but it is the only way I know how to do it. I've slept in my car a lot of times, and that really messes with your head.

"I can't play what other people want me to play. I've got to do it my way. But it sure ain't easy. I don't plan my future much past my next song.

"The sacrifices never stop in this business. You think things can't get worse, but they do somehow. But you've got to give it your all and take the chance.

"My music is the most important thing in the world to me. It is a way of expressing myself, the only way I have. When I'm up there singing, I'm revealing things about myself that have never been revealed before.

"It was hard to be that honest for a long time. Used to, I wouldn't sing unless they turned the lights down, but I've gotten more self-confidence now. I'm my own worst critic, and it has only been in the last two years when I thought I was good enough to make it."

Reagan's part of the show ends after 45 minutes. He comes off, drenched in sweat, his eyes bright with the fever.

"Being out there is like being high," he said, trying to catch his breath and come back to Earth. "It's like you're floating. Everybody in the band was clicking tonight.

"That's what keeps you going. That's what it's all about."

The last echoes of his song have faded, but the last line lingers on, hanging over the goodtime crowd like a plea from his heart, "Don't give up believing in me."

When Life's Work Is Burned

Leggett

There were 12,000 house fires in North Carolina in 1980, the last year for which statistics are available, causing an estimated $150 million in damages.

Twelve thousand fires are a statistic; one fire is a tragedy.

This is the story of one house fire and what it means to lose everything you have worked for all your life.

Booger was the first cat Dennis Coker had ever liked. He'd always been a dog man before, but there was something about the feisty kitten that he admired.

Booger was standing by the door when Dennis, 22, and Cathy, his 20-year-old wife, left their house near Leggett at 7:45 a.m. one January day. Their big white dog Zeigh was on the screened-in side porch.

Dennis and Cathy were running late. Dennis was supposed to be at his job as a mechanic in nearby Tarboro at 8 a.m. and Cathy, eight months pregnant with their first child, was going to drive him to work and then take the car to keep a routine doctor's appointment.

They didn't look back when they drove away from the rambling farm house under the big trees. They wish they had.

The next person to notice the house was a traveling salesman. He drove by about an hour later and saw smoke. He must have thought it was a big fire in the fireplace because he didn't stop.

Dennis and Cathy Coker's house was on fire. Within two hours they would lose everything they had, including the kitten named Booger.

The salesman stopped at Jack Andrews' store down the road in Lawrence and mentioned that he had seen a lot of smoke coming from a house. Jack questioned him and figured out which house it was. He called David Coker, Dennis' brother and a volunteer firefighter, to go check it out.

Events moved rapidly then, but the fire moved faster.

David's mother alerted Barry Pittman Jr., Dennis and Cathy's nearest neighbor and himself a firefighter.

Zeigh tried to do her job as a watchdog and growled when Barry tried to get near the house. He calmed her down enough to investigate. He gave the alarm by radio. It was 9:10 a.m. and the fire was growing hotter.

Leggett volunteer firefighters, monitoring their radios, began gathering before David and a fire truck arrived on the scene from town, four miles away.

"The back porch was in flames when I got there," David said. "The house was full of smoke. I broke a window to reach in and open the door and the lock had melted. It was hot in there."

The firefighters ran two hoses and began trying to save Dennis and Cathy's house.

Dennis was at work, installing an oil pump in a Buick, when he got the call. It was his sister Michelle on the phone.

"You'd better go home," she said. "Your house is on fire."

Bill Allsbrook, Dennis' boss, had overhead enough of the conversation to know what was happening. As soon as Dennis hung up the phone, Allsbrook handed him a set of car keys and a license plate for a new car and told him to go.

"I though I'd never get there," Dennis said of the 10-mile trip. "The whole way I was praying it was just around the chimney.

"I drove 70 all the way to Leggett, and when I got there I could see the smoke. I knew then there wouldn't be much left. Then I drove 90."

David and firefighters from four rual departments were trying to contain the fire, but they were losing the fight.

"It makes a difference when it is your brother's house," said David, 18, and a firefighter for two years. "I went into the house without an air-pack to try to stop it.

"We got the back porch under control, but the fire had gotten into the attic. That's when we lost it."

Dennis Coker also is a firefighter. He had just joined the department, and the first house fire he fought was his own.

"The kitchen and the back porch were gone when I got there," Dennis said. "There was a lot of flame in the back and smoke everywhere else.

"I ran around to the back of the house and drove my pickup away from the door. Then I put on my gear and tried to help, but it is hard to fight a fire when you have tears in your eyes.

"I knew I was going to lose a lot of it because it kept getting worse.

"I put on an air-pack and went inside. You couldn't see your hand in front of your face. You couldn't even see the flames, they were just orange glows in the smoke.

"As soon as the fire died down some I went back inside to get our wedding pictures. I knew I could replace everything else but I couldn't replace those pictures. My mother had always said that if her house burned, her pictures would be the one thing she'd want to save and I thought of that.

"I found the picture album in some rubble. The cover was burned but most of the wedding pictures were saved.

"But I couldn't find Booger anywhere. He had no way out of the house. Zeigh was all right, she knew how to get off the porch, but Booger was gone. That hurt the most.

"I found myself just standing out there, watching my home burn. I didn't say anything, I just felt numb.

"I was waiting for Cathy to get there. I wanted to be there when she drove up."

• • •

As Cathy listened to the doctor that mid-January morning, she didn't know that her plans were to be changed forever.

"I was happy when I left the doctor's office," she said, "I went by where Dennis worked to tell him that everything was OK. He wasn't there, and they wouldn't tell me where he was. They told me to go to my mother's house."

At that moment, Dennis Coker was standing in the ruins of their house.

"We'd lived in some bad places," Dennis said. "We lived in a trailer at first and even lived in the back of funeral home for a while. I hated that. This was our fifth house in 18 months. We loved it here.

"It's tough when you're young and trying to get started. You scrimp and do without a lot of things. Just the night before the fire, we were talking about how much we had managed to accumulate for the baby. Of course, all of that went up in the fire."

Confused and frightened, Cathy went to her mother's house, and there she learned of the fire.

"They didn't want me to go, figuring I'd go into labor, but after a few minutes I went anyway," Cathy said.

Dennis was standing in the front yard when she drove up, heartbroken and grimy from fighting the fire.

"Cathy got out of the car and I went over to her," he said. "Both of us were crying. I put my arms around her and told her that everything would be all right.

"But I didn't believe it when I said it."

"And I didn't believe it when he said it either," Cathy said.

Dennis went back inside the house "after everything was over," he said. "I managed to get a few dishes, the frame of our wood stove and my shotgun. Someone else had pulled a chest out of a front room, but I don't know if it will ever be usable.

"I also found a box in a front bedroom that had some jeans in it. We wear the same size, and we'd bought several pair. Cathy wouldn't let me wear them all because she wanted some of them for when after the baby came and she could get in them again. That, and the clothes on our back, were all we had left."

The young couple moved in with Dennis' parents while they tried to figure out what to do next. Then their community opened its heart.

"I couldn't believe what happened," Dennis said. "People started bringing us things. I've never seen so many clothes in my life. Most of it was good stuff but, to be honest, some people did want us to take their junk off their hands.

"We ended up with more clothes that we had before the fire.

"A furniture store donated us a great dinette set. The Red Cross in Tarboro helped us buy a new stove and refrigerator. People brought us chairs and tables and more maternity clothes then you can imagine."

Most of the donations came from neighbors, but some were from total strangers, people touched by the plight of a young couple burned out.

"I didn't know it would be like this," Dennis said. "I knew we had friends, but I didn't know how many and I didn't know strangers would do something like this for us.

"Nothing good ever comes from a fire. Both of us were pretty depressed after it happened. We'd lost everything, there had even been a baby shower for Cathy and all those presents burned. Her suitcase that we kept packed for when it was time for the baby burned.

"But something like this teaches you a lot about people and how good they really are.

"We're going to stay here. We're going to find another house to live in and we'll get more furniture and we'll be all right.

"I wouldn't leave here now if I could. I feel like I ought to stay here and do something nice for these people.

"I've heard people say they know how we feel, losing everything in a fire, but they don't until it happens to them.

"I'm a fireman and the next time I go fight a fire at somebody's house I will be able to say that and mean it.

"I do know how it feels to lose it all.

"It hurts, it hurts a lot."

Truck Theft More Than Routine

"I know it was just a truck, just a hunk of metal," Perry Matthews said. "And I haven't cried about it being stolen.

"But I sure wanted to."

Stolen vehicles are not big news. It happens all the time. There were 422 vehicles stolen in Raleigh in 1981, according to the Raleigh Police Department, so it is more than a daily occurrence.

But it is big news when it happens to you.

"After I realized it was stolen, I just stood at the window and stared out at the parking place," said Matthews, a construction welder. "All I could think about was somebody riding in my truck. My truck.

"That truck was a big part of my life. I started saving for it when I was 10 years old. My mother started me a bank account with $5 in 1970, and I did everything I could to make money to put in the bank.

"I mowed lawns, and as I got older I learned how to repair machinery. I did everything. My father ran a landscaping business, and I learned how to repair his machinery and keep it going. I used to plow gardens for people, and I always saved my money. I didn't know what I wanted at first, but by the time I was 15 I knew I wanted a pickup truck.

"All my friends wanted cars. I was the only one who wanted a pickup.

"When I was 16, I had about $4,000 saved, and I talked to the salesman for five weeks before he'd give me the price I could afford. Even then I had to borrow a little bit from my daddy, but I worked and paid him back.

"I always believed in working for what you got. I didn't go to town except on Saturday night. Every night I was out working in the shop. My friends knew if I wasn't downtown by 9 p.m. on Saturday to come out to the shop. I'd be out there working.

"My friends used to make fun of me, but I loved my truck, and I took good care of it. You know, some girls didn't want to date you if you didn't have a good car, but I figured any girl who didn't want to date me in my pickup truck I shouldn't bother with.

"Everybody in Thomasville knew me because of my truck. They might not know my name, but they knew the boy in the green pickup. It was a four-wheel drive before they were popular, and it had big tires that made a lot of noise when they rolled.

"My Mama would lay in bed waiting for me to come home at night, and when she heard those big tires rolling up to the house she knew she could go to sleep; her boy was home.

"There used to be a place up in the Uwharrie National Forest I'd go when something was bothering me. I'd sit there in my truck and look out at the view, and I'd think it all out. I always felt good there, sitting in my truck, especially in the spring."

One girl didn't mind riding in Perry's pickup. Her name is Terry, she's from Lexington and she's married to Perry. They're expecting their first child.

"My Mama and I wanted a big wedding," she said. "Perry couldn't understand it, but he went along with everything but one. I wanted to leave the reception in my aunt's Lincoln Continental but Perry wouldn't do it. He told me that the truck had been such a part of our lives that he wanted it in the wedding, so we left the reception in that pickup.

"And when we flew back in from our honeymoon, the first thing he said was, 'There's my pickup, it's all right.' "

The last ride Perry took in his pickup was to buy lumber early this month so he could build his baby's cradle.

"I remember stopping in the parking lot, and looking back at my truck that night," he said. "It looked good, and I thought then that I hoped it would be as good in the future as it had been.

"I came home and backed it in the parking place out front and locked it."

That was the last time he saw it. It could have been there the next morning, but he didn't notice when he left at 6 a.m. to drive his old jalopy to work.

"I didn't drive my truck to work," he said. "There were too many maniacs in that parking lot to leave my truck there all day."

It was that afternoon when he found it was missing, and Lord how it hurt.

"We looked around, and in the bushes we found the springs to the baby's bed and the floor mats," he said. "And I found the lock to the passenger's side. They ripped that out to get inside. That's all I have left now of my pickup."

He sat there in their little apartment and looked down at the lock for a moment, just a broken hunk of metal you could put in your pocket.

"It makes you sick when it happens," he said. "I've always believed that a man should work for what he gets. I've always tried to be honest, and then somebody steals my truck. It seems like the honest man is always the victim.

"It has taken me a long time to get over it, and I'm not completely over it yet. I was hostile to everybody. I was suspicious of everyone. I wanted to take my hostility out on everyone. It even affected our relationship until Terry sat me down and talked to me.

"I want my truck back even if it is in a million pieces. Terry and I have had to work for everything we've had, and we could work to get it fixed up again. There wasn't any insurance on it, so we're just out.

"We'll have another truck. It'll take a while, but we'll have another one, but it won't ever be the same."

The police say the green 1975 Chevrolet pickup with a white top, N.C. license number AL 7181, probably was stolen by professionals and have told Perry that the chances of getting it back are slim.

But if you happen to see it somewhere, I know a nice fellow who'd like to have it back.

Taking On All Comers

Edenton

He was out on the edge, just a nudge away from pure rage.

"It ain't right," he said. "It just ain't right."

There are people in Edenton who would like nothing more than to wake up one morning and find it was all a bad dream, that Emmett Wiggins, who has tormented them for decades, wasn't really out there in the bushes, lying in wait for them, waiting for his chance to chew on them like a determined bulldog.

There also are people in Edenton who admire him as a cantankerous scrapper, a man perfectly willing to take on anyone or anything for the sheer exuberance of doing what "they" say can't be done.

"If a man don't love a challenge, what kind of man is he?" Wiggins said. "I enjoy it."

He has fought the storms often enough, the storms that blow in from the Atlantic and the backroom storms that swirl through small towns.

There is the lawsuit, first of all, a lawsuit that has been in court for 31 years. Wiggins, somewhat proudly, says it is the longest-running suit in Chowan County history.

I would not presume to explain or take sides in the suit. Simply put, Wiggins says he owns 1,500 acres of land that the state says it owns.

"I've been through 18 lawyers on this thing," he said. "It ain't right the way I've been treated. That land is mine. How many times have I got to pay for it? But I'll fight them until I'm dead."

That is no idle boast. Wiggins believes with all his heart that he is right, and when he believes in something, he fights.

He fought in July 1980 when he salvaged several tons of marble from the bottom of the Atlantic Ocean. The marble had been there since 1895, when the bark Clythia mistook False Cape for Cape Henry at the entrance to Chesapeake Bay. The bark ran aground and sank with 1,100 tons of statuary marble from Genoa, Italy, bound for Baltimore. Wiggins salvaged the marble simply because he thought he could do it and it seemed like an interesting challenge.

Then there is his house. Wiggins lives in the only lighthouse in North Carolina. I know what you're thinking. You're thinking that those black and white towers along the coast are lighthouses, but they aren't. They are merely towers with lights. Wiggins' house, which at one time served ships entering the Roanoke River from Albemarle Sound, has a light on the roof.

He thought it would be nice to have the house, so he moved it, by water, to Edenton.

"I brought her in on the barge and tied up at the county dock at the foot of Main Street," he said.

The town, of course, was agog.

Wiggins, it must be said, has a cheeky sense of humor to accompany his individualistic flair. Several years ago, he acquired a battered tugboat that had sunk in Albemarle Sound in 1971. He moored it in front of his house, and some folks immediately hauled him into court, saying the old tug was simply too ugly. Visual pollution, they screamed.

Wiggins lost his court battle and was ordered to remove the tug by Oct. 31, 1981. But then he got sick and couldn't do it, and besides he said, drought had left the water level too low to float it into the channel.

Back he went to court, charged with disobeying a court order. This time he fought, won and got all his court costs back.

Then he moved the tug from his yard — and moored it next to the Edenton police station, where everyone could see it better.

The tug itself is another story. It was salvaged shortly after it sank in 1971. Other people worked on it for years and spent a lot of money before giving up and selling the 100-foot steel boat to Wiggins for $1,000. Of course, they told him, it couldn't be moved, because it was hemmed in by a sandbar, and it never would run again. The engine was shot.

But he moved it and began working on it with a friend, Larry Hartley. The tug that never would put to sea again put to sea with Hartley coaxing the 21-foot-long diesel engine to life and Wiggins at the wheel. It was rusty and battle-scarred. The engine controls from the bridge were a jerry-rigged bunch of cables operated by hand, but the mighty Maryland sailed proudly into Edenton Bay.

A salvage diver, a tugboat captain, the first water skier in Edenton, the pilot of his own seaplane, the man who raised the Civil War cannons of Fort Branch from the waters of the Roanoke River, the salvage expert who brought up a sunken freighter fully loaded with coal — all of these are Emmett Wiggins.

At 61, he isn't about to roll over and play dead for anyone.

He's got this idea for an engine that, basically, would use water for fuel, and if he can just get his hands on some of those tiles used to insulate the space shuttle, he'll be in business.

"What I'd love to do is restore that old tugboat and put my seaplane on the aft deck and take off," he said.

Sure as he did, like Don Quixote he would find another battle to fight somewhere.

Tale of a Turtle and a Maid

Havelock

Once upon a time in a fairytale land, a lovely maiden kissed an ugly frog.

The enchanted frog magically turned into a handsome prince, and they lived happily ever after.

Once upon a time on a real college campus, a fair maiden named Alice kissed an ugly turtle, and she was even luckier. Her turtle stayed a turtle, and they still live happily ever after.

Draw your little chairs closer, kiddies, and I shall tell you the tale of the remarkable adventures of Butch the turtle and Alice, the fair maiden who loved him.

Butch is not an ordinary turtle. He is a Red-Eared Slider. Isn't that an awful name, boys and girls? I'll bet you didn't even know turtles had ears, did you?

Butch was real little, like you, when he first met Alice. He was so little, he could sit on a quarter.

Alice, the fair maiden in our story, was a student at St. Mary's College in Raleigh when her roommate, Anne Zuhling, gave her Butch and another turtle as an Easter present in 1970. Most people would have thrown their roommates out the window if they had been given a turtle for Easter, but Alice just smiled and smiled. Alice likes turtles.

Butch was a criminal turtle. Turtles were not allowed in a St. Mary's room in 1970. But then, neither were boys or hairdryers, and since Butch did not use electricity or drink beer, no one complained.

Butch lived in a little plastic bowl with a little plastic palm tree. I'm not going to tell you what happened to Butch's little turtle friend. Take it from me, you don't want to know.

Alice and Butch became close friends. Butch went home to Rocky Mount with Alice every weekend, where he was, at best, tolerated by Alice's patient parents, who still remembered the time that Sambo the rabbit had eaten all of Alice's mother's pink petunias. So they kept a close eye on Butch, although how many petunias could a turtle the size of a quarter eat?

Butch and Alice had lived together for a year when Butch, who had dreams of being an athlete, entered his first turtle race at Myrtle Beach, where he and Alice were spending the summer.

Butch did not win his first and only race. Some people say Butch did win, but a little boy who had his turtle in the race started crying, so they gave the bright blue ribbon to the little boy.

Butch loved Alice very much, so much that even after Alice was arrested for dancing around the grave of a dead woman as a college prank, Butch remained her best friend.

Then one day, a terrible thing happened. Butch and Alice were separated. Alice and Butch were living at home, and it was decided that the best thing for Butch would be for him to live at the Rocky Mount Children's Museum.

The good people at the museum found a nice home for Butch. It had a lot of water and a place to crawl around.

It also had a lot of alligators.

One day, an alligator got real hungry and munched on Butch like you do on a cookie. Butch looked awful. His bottom was battered and his top was torn. It was a dark day for turtledom.

That's when Alice said "enough is enough" and brought Butch home. Alice and husband Henry doctored Butch as best they could, and, lo, Butch bounced back.

But there were other exciting adventures to come for Butch and Alice. Butch went blind one time when big ugly things grew over his eyes.

Blind Butch, who became the only turtle in the world with a seeing-eye fair maiden, was visiting in Tennessee when the miracle happened. He was sunning on the car roof, his favorite place, when he scratched the yucky things on his eyes and one of them fell off. Then the other one fell off, and Alice was so happy. So was Butch, I'm sure.

Butch kept growing and growing, and one day when he was a grown-up turtle about the size of a dinner plate, he ran away to explore the world. Oh, it was wonderful fun. Alice and Henry looked under rocks, and they looked under piles of leaves, but Butch was nowhere to be found.

He had been gone five days when, one day, Alice was out sweeping the patio and thinking of her long-lost friend.

Suddenly, there was a rustle in the garden. Whatever could it be? Alice looked up, and there came Butch, back from his world tour at a gallop.

Well, it wasn't a gallop. It was more like a slow crawl, but this is a fairytale.

Butch was all dried out, and turtles don't like to be all dried out, so when Alice put him in his tub of water, he stretched out, smiled and sighed. He was home with fair Alice, never to roam again.

Butch is 13 now and lives in a little swimming pool all summer and a washtub all winter at the parsonage of St. Christopher's Episcopal Church in Havelock, where Henry is the rector.

He still has scars from his fight with the mean old alligator and sometimes looks longingly at the horizon (for a turtle, that isn't all that far), but he seems happy.

And Alice Proctor Witten, the fair maiden, who lives in a house with two dogs, two cats, two gerbils, two sons, two rabbits, one husband and one turtle, still loves him.

How's that for a happy ending, boys and girls?

Not Much Romance on the Road

Albemarle

Sometimes, late at night, Brooks Wilson lies in his bed and listens to the lonesome sound of a distant train, and he remembers.

"You'd get mighty hungry, thirsty and cold out there on the road," he said. "I've had to keep moving to keep from freezing to death, and I've been in the desert all day and all night with no food and water.

"I hear those trains, and I'm glad I'm not out there anymore.

"When I think back now, there was some romance to the road, but really most of it was pretty bad."

Brooks Wilson, 77, knows about the road. From 1922 to 1935 he was a hobo. He is quick to point out that he wasn't a bum or a tramp, he was a part of a proud breed, the Knights of the Road, the men who rode the rails.

"A hobo would work if he could, a tramp wouldn't work, and a bum was so sorry he couldn't work," he said. "I was a hobo. We had rules of the road."

Brooks Wilson is more than just an old hobo. He is Hobo No. 1, chosen by his peers at the 74th annual Hobo Jamboree in Birmingham, Ala., and has a personalized license plate reading "Hobo 1" to prove it.

He left his home in Reidsville in 1922.

"My mama was dead, and I had no home," he said. "One day I was in the Spencer yards and thought, 'I know what I'll do.' I jumped a freight and took off. I was scared to death. I was 17."

He rode for 13 years, covering 46 of the 48 states (he didn't get to Idaho and Washington), living life as best he could.

"I've walked up to many a door and asked, 'Sir, if you have anything left from supper I'd sure appreciate it, and if you've got any work that needs doing, I'll be glad to do it,' " he said. "I never in my life said, 'Buddy, can you spare a dime?' Those people were bums.

"And I never even thought of robbing anybody. Now I've been chased out of a lot of peach and apple orchards and watermelon fields, but I never stole a thing but a few kisses — and I always paid those back."

He lived in the hobo jungles and took his baths in cold creeks.

"I never tried to look like a hobo," he said. "I carried soap, a razor and a towel along with a change of pants and a shirt. I'd carry it all wrapped in newspaper and hung across my back so I'd have both hands free to hop a train."

Getting on a train moving faster than you can run is not easy.

"I've seen hoboes get their legs cut off," he said. "I've seen some awful sights."

The cold and the hunger and the loneliness were bad enough, but the real terrors were the railroad bulls, the security men hired to keep hoboes off the trains.

"The worst was the Atlantic Coast Line," he said. "They had a reputation that no hobo could ride their trains, and Hamlet was the worst town of all. Now a bull was supposed to keep you off, but he wasn't supposed to hurt you. But most of them did. I once hopped a train in Hamlet to prove I could do it.

"There were some famous bulls. There was Hobo Brown between Charlotte and Greenville, South Carolina, who dressed like a hobo and was one of the meanest.

"There was One-Arm Kelly in Mobile. He had a hook. He got after me a lot, but I always got away.

"But the worst was Texas Slim out in Longview, Texas. If he caught you, you pulled 60 days on a chain gang. In Florida it was 90 days, but I never pulled a day in jail.

"All bulls had a gun in one hand and a rubber hose in the other. I ran from them. I've been 'caught at' but never caught."

Sometimes he rode the rails looking for work. Sometimes he rode because there was nothing else to do.

"I didn't care how long it took to get somewhere," he said. "I didn't have no appointments to keep.

"One time I went from Philadelphia to Los Angeles in 11 days and made it back in 13. That was moving pretty good.

"One time I got put off in the desert in June and walked a day and a half with no food and water. A lot of men died out there on those roads.

" I consider myself lucky to be alive today. It never entered my mind that an old hobo like me would be living in his own house and not owe a penny."

He left the road in 1935 when he got a full-time job with Alcoa in nearby Badin and stayed with it until he retired. He never regretted his decision to leave the hobo life behind.

"There was a fellow who used to think the hobo life was romantic," he said. "He always wanted to go with me, but I didn't want to start anybody hoboing. I'd tell him I'd take him and we would be leaving on a particular day. Then I'd leave the day before.

"I guess if I'd never done it, I'd think it was romantic, too.

"I still like to look at the trains when they go through, but I never see a hobo anymore. I'd like to see one just to see what they look like now.

"I don't ever want to be a hobo again, but if I had to, I could. I'd have to catch slower trains this time, but a hobo never forgets."

Super Grit Cowboy Band

Bailey

Clyde Mattocks slumped in his chair in the recording studio, rubbing his forehead and searching for the sound in his mind.

"Do it again," he said. "The texture ain't right yet."

Stonewall crowded the microphone and sang it again, looking for the right way to make what could be a silly song into something personal, real and heartbreaking — the way a good country song has to be.

" I don't know what it is, but I'll know it when I hear it," Clyde said.

Stonewall kept singing and singing. Finally, Clyde sat up in his chair in the Mega Sound Studios control room and said, "I like that."

And it was done. One more song by the Super Grit Cowboy Band was ready for the new album.

"Somebody has to be the SOB," Clyde said. "In our band that's me."

"Clyde makes those decisions for us," drummer and singer Danny "Stonewall" Vinson said. "There is no one who knows more about our kind of music than Clyde. Right or wrong, we go with him."

Feelings are hurt easily on the honky-tonk trail of North Carolina's home-grown music. Bands are struggling for bookings in a depressed economy, recording contracts are hard to come by and artists are the kind of people who take slights, real and imagined, very seriously.

But you can ask any of the country pickers, booking agents or bar owners, and they'll all tell you the same thing: Clyde Mattocks, a 45-year-old former kitchen appliance repairman from Kinston and leader of Super Grit, is the most respected man and musican of the talented lot.

Mattocks is to "Carolina Country Boogie" — the state's own upbeat blend of country and rock — what Willie Nelson once was to the country music outlaws of Texas.

He has been picking and singing in roadhouses and honky-tonks for 30 years, since the working men of East Caswell Street in Kinston took a few minutes and showed their young neighbor some hot licks in the early '50s.

"One night a guy came over with a pedal steel guitar," Clyde said during a break in the recording session. "I'd never seen one. I heard him play, and I knew that was the sound I had been attracted to. I knew right then that's what I wanted to do."

He played in a lot of bands along the way, including one period in the late '50s when he played on two local television shows. He played steel with Smiley O'Brien's band on one station and with Jim Thorton's band on another.

By 1974, he had reached the point where he could make enough money in the honky-tonks to give up his appliance repair business, but it wasn't a particularly happy time.

"I was pretty disillusioned with Nashville's country music," he said. "And I still am."

Clyde was looking for an alternative to the over-produced, too-slick, syrupy Nashville sound that was popular then and now. One night he went to a Dirt Band concert in Wilson, and it all changed.

"I thought to myself that I was playing for the wrong kind of people," he said. "Those young folks were having fun."

Clyde had found his music, a let-her-rip marriage of traditional country and full-tilt rock 'n' roll, and the Super Grit Cowboy Band hit the state running. It hasn't mellowed or slowed.

"The country clubs didn't know how to take us, and the rock 'n' roll clubs didn't know how to take us," he said. "We became country's favorite rock 'n' roll band and rock 'n' roll's favorite country band."

And it has worked, better and longer than anyone expected. The band — consisting of Clyde "Loose Lester" Mattocks on pedal steel, banjo and guitar, Curtis "Blue" Wright on guitar, Mike "13" Kinzey on fiddle, keyboard and tuba (yes, tuba), Allen "Wizard" Hicks on guitar and Danny "Stonewall" Vinson on drums — plays for a quarter of a million people a year and has played twice with the East Carolina Symphony.

It is a raucous, good-time band, blending bluegrass fire, country weepers and rock 'n' roll passion into a show that makes the Saturday kickers and cowboys whoop it up and drink 'em down. Only the dead don't boogie with Super Grit.

"I won't take credit for it all," Clyde said. "If I've done anything, it is to make bands not ashamed to play traditional country music.

"I know we're good, but Nashville says our hair's too long, we're too scruffy looking, we don't sound right. They want us to do what everyone else is doing. The music business is reflective, not progressive. They want something that sounds like what's hot right now.

"I'd rather for us to be known as a band that lasted 10 years with a loyal following than to be this year's hot-shot band that sold out to get there. I've got to live with myself.

"There is a lot of good music out there that isn't being played on the radio. We give them that alternative.

"I promised these boys they'd make a living with the band, not that they'd be stars. Funny thing is, Nashville tells us what we ought to do, and then we outdraw the bands they send to this area.

"We play for a million people, too, but we do it face to face, 200 people at the time. I want to play for the people who pay their money and come out to a bar on Saturday night. They're the best critics. They understand us."

A Family Too Tough to Quit

Cedar Creek

The Robinson family is as tough as leather. That's good, because what has happened to them would destroy weaker people.

They came to this back-country high ground east of Cedar Creek in southeastern Cumberland County 100 years ago. No one is sure how they got there or where they came from, but once they arrived, they put their roots into the sandy soil and stayed.

It was hard times. Black families trying to hold onto their land in the South have had to work hard to do it, and no family worked harder than the Robinsons.

"This is a family place," Elbert Robinson said. "As each generation came along, they built a house here."

There were 11 houses in the Robinson family compound before the tornado hit. Now there are none.

Everything for which the Robinson family worked for a century is gone. All the houses were demolished, and their Uncle Harvey Robinson, one of the senior brothers of the close-knit family, is dead.

"You can't run from God," said John Erwin Robinson, 61, Harvey's brother. "I've been here all my life, and if the good Lord spares me, I'll rebuild."

I asked Elbert Robinson to call the family roll and tell what had happened to them at 7:02 p.m., March 28, 1984:

"My first cousin Sue Clark lived in the first house. It's gone.

"Kenneth McNair, my first cousin's husband, lived in the next house. It will have to be torn down to the floors and rebuilt.

"My father lived next door to me, and you can see there is nothing left but a bonfire.

"My first cousin Winfred Robinson lived in a trailer. You can't see that anymore.

"My Uncle Harvey lived in the next house, and he was killed. His wife is still in the hospital.

"Then there was Lewis Robinson in a trailer and David Robinson in a trailer, and they're both gone.

"Then there was my grandmother, Mrs. Maggie Cooper. She's the oldest one, and her house is gone.

"John Robinson Jr. lived next to her, and Donald Robinson lived in a trailer next to him. Their places are gone.

"I can count 33 people who are homeless just from our family, and I know I've left out some."

Eleven houses. Thirty-three people. And that is just one family on a half-mile stretch of country road.

The Robinson family always has made its living by working hard as brickmasons.

"We all started working together in the summer carrying cement, sand and bricks in wheelbarrows," Elbert said. "My father and my uncles would teach each of us how to lay brick, and we all stayed with it.

"We all pulled together all of the time. We're a close family, and we've had some good times and some bad times out here. This is one of the bad times."

Elbert never will forget the night it happened, the night a fearsome storm tried to destroy the entire family and failed.

"I was coming around the curve when I saw my house blow apart and fly across the swamp," Elbert said. "It picked my car up six feet off the ground and turned it 180 degrees and slammed it back on the road.

"I was crying and trembling and praying to God. I knew my wife and boy were in that house. Fire was jumping out of all the power lines that were down, but I knew I had to go in and get them out.

"My wife had heard the warning on television, and she and my boy were talking about what to do if it came. She said they ought to get under the bed, but he said they ought to get in the closet.

"They went into his bedroom and were taking the clothes out of the closet when they heard it. They dived into the closet and shut the door and fell on their knees and started praying. That's where I found them. That corner with the closet was the only thing standing.

"I ran out and started calling for my mother and father next door. I heard them answer, and I went on down the line trying to find my family.

"I found my Uncle Harvey. He was hurt real bad, and he said, 'Don't worry about me, I'm digging my way to heaven.'

"I knelt there in the rain, holding his head in my lap, crying and packing wet sand on him to stop the bleeding. But he died.

"About that time, a Trailways bus came up, and we got everybody together on the bus as we found them. The people were so nice. Some of the family was getting ready for bed and were in their underwear, and the people on the bus opened their luggage to dress them. We took care of everybody until the ambulances started arriving.

"The family is all over the area now, staying with friends and other family, but we're coming back home. I don't know how we'll do it, but we will. We're too tough to quit.

"You know, I laid the first brick in this house myself right in that corner. I'm going to save that brick and it will be the first brick in the new house.

"This family has been here too long. We've got to keep the faith and this family together. We'll just back up, regroup and hold our heads up and roll on."

Elbert's son walked up holding a tin of fish hooks in his hand. He had found them in the wreckage and knew his daddy liked to fish. He wanted to make his daddy feel better.

"Thanks, son," Elbert said with a smile. "But we can't go fishing now. We've got work to do."

A Memorable First Anniversary

Faison

He wanted to make sure it would be a wedding anniversary she would never forget.

He succeeded beyond his wildest dreams.

"Forget it?" she said. "I can't stop thinking about it. And I blush every time. I can't believe he told you about it. I'm going to wring his neck."

Then, as promised, she blushed and hit him a solid love tap on his shoulder. He grinned like a possum eating persimmons and hugged her. Then she beamed.

For reasons that shall shortly become obvious, I promised the couple I would not publish their names.

Goodness knows, true love is hard enough to find, and I'm not going to do anything to make these two lovers mad at each other. Or at me.

I think all of us will remember Wednesday, March 28, 1984. We may not remember the exact date in years to come, but we will be telling our children's children about the day the tornadoes came to Eastern North Carolina.

The couple will remember it, but I wonder what they will tell their children when they ask, "What were you doing that night?"

Their story begins early Wednesday morning. It was their first wedding anniversary, and they were being secretive about the plans for that night. But you can bet they both had big plans.

Her anniversary present to him was a new shotgun. She had carefully wrapped it, and while he was taking his morning shower, she went out to the car and brought it inside and hid it under the bed.

They both went off to work.

He left work early that day to pick up her present.

It was a brand new pickup truck.

OK, so it wasn't diamonds or a trip to Paris, but she grew up driving pickup trucks and she liked them. Besides, she needed something new to drive because her old car was ready for Automobile Heaven. And she's a country girl.

"I got home and parked her truck about a quarter of a mile from the house, down behind a barn next to the woods so she couldn't see it," he said. "I made it back to the house just before she got home."

It was late in the afternoon, and the murderous tornadoes were building over South Carolina and heading their way.

Dinner was going to be wonderful. They spent a few minutes just talking, and then they both dressed up for dinner. He put on a nice sport coat, and she put on a long, fancy dress.

Dinner was steaks and wine by candlelight, just the two of them, so much in love and so happy they were about to bust.

They dawdled over dinner, and then she got up and brought him his present. He unwrapped his new shotgun and was delighted.

"This crazy fool went out and shot a limb off a tree just to see how it worked," she said.

The tornadoes had hit Bennettsville, S.C., and were getting closer.

Then it was time for her present.

He told her to come with him. She naturally asked where they were going, and he told her to hush up and come on. It was getting really cloudy and rainy-looking outside, and they had to hurry.

They walked the quarter of a mile down the path to the old barn. She took her shoes off and walked barefooted, her long, fancy dress brushing the weeds. They walked hand in hand.

"I couldn't figure out what in the world he was doing," she said.

He made her close her eyes as they got to the barn. He led her carefully around the barn and then, with the new truck in plain sight with a bright blue ribbon tied to the door and the words, "I love you" written in water paint on the new windshield, he told her to open her eyes.

"I screamed and started jumping up and down and laughing," she said. "It was so pretty."

But he wasn't through, not by a country mile.

He told her to get in the driver's side, and he climbed in the passenger side.

Inside the truck was a small cooler. She opened the cooler and there was a bottle of champagne, two glasses and a candle.

"That's when I started crying," she said. "It was the sweetest thing."

But there was one more surprise, and this is where it gets a little delicate.

He had plans, you see. He wanted to make sure that every time she got in that truck she'd think of him and the night of their first anniversary.

Think about it. A young couple, married only a year, a little giddy from a bottle of wine and now a glass of champagne, total privacy, deeply in love, a soft kiss, candlelight, a night to remember.

If this were a movie, the camera would now pan out the window. We shall do the same.

A little while later the storm hit.

They were in no danger. The tornado was a mile or so away, and they didn't see it. But the wind blew hard, and the rain and hail came in buckets.

"I looked out and could see that an old tree had fallen across the path," he said. "I said we might as well stay right there until it quit raining, so we did."

So there they stayed, in the now unforgettable front seat of her new pickup, sipping champagne and giggling the storm away.

It was good they didn't know about the tornado. Nothing should have spoiled that night.

And nothing did.

Ricky Lamm Beats the Odds

Wilson

Jo Ann Lamm admits it wasn't easy.

"At first I'd stand at the door and look at the other children in the neighborhood and say, 'Why me?'

"Then one day I caught myself saying, 'Thank you, Lord.' That's when I know Ricky was a blessing.'"

And it was then that the miracle began.

And now, 26 years later, her eyes fill with tears when she tries to talk about the achievements of her son, Ricky. She's so proud she can hardly stand it.

Ricky didn't have much going for him at first. He was born prematurely, weighing only 4 pounds at birth. He spent 31 days in an incubator, a month that saved his life but left his brain damaged. Nothing would ever change that.

Some school officials said he shouldn't enter the first grade, that he could never learn.

Specialists told her that Ricky was a hopeless case and told Jo Ann and her husband J.T. to "take him home and love him and take care of him."

So you can imagine how proud she is when she talks about Ricky, recently named the 1982 Employee of the Year at the Coca-Cola Bottling Company of Wilson.

Earl Harrison, the assistant plant manager, said of Ricky: "He is one of the most conscientious employees I know. If anyone should be called Mr. Coca-Cola, it is Ricky. If we've ever had a faithful employee, he's the one.

"When he came to work here six years age, he couldn't even sweep the floor by himself. He had to learn by watching someone else.

"Now he gives us an honest day's work. He earns his pay. He does as much with what he's got as anyone here. I've never seen an employee more loyal to the company. He is most deserving of being our Employee of the Year."

And Ricky loves it.

"It has been a long, hard struggle," Ricky said. "But I pulled through it. Coca-Cola gave me a chance to work and to prove I could do it.

"It was hard, but I had to really watch and try to do it on my own. If you want something, you have to prove to yourself and to your employers that you can do it. People should realize the value of working."

Mrs. Lamm says that working at Coca-Cola has been "the most wonderful thing that could have happened to Ricky."

"I could never have dreamed he would make this kind of progress," she said. "When Ricky was born, people hid kids like him in the closet, but once I accepted the situation, I knew I could either hide him or say: 'Hey world, here he is. He's my son, and if you don't like him, then you don't like me.'

"I never blamed anyone for what happened. It was an accident, but life is like a puzzle, and Ricky is one part of that puzzle."

Ricky went to school for 12 years in Wilson. He spent two years in the first grade, two in the second, and then a special education teacher named Georgia Martin took him under her wing and taught him for five years.

"She had a lot to do with it," Mrs. Lamm said. "She helped Ricky an awful lot."

Mrs. Lamm couldn't work outside her home because of Ricky so she opened a nursery in her home. Having Ricky around made her do a better job at it, she says.

"Ricky taught me that little children are all different people, all with different needs," she said. "You can't treat them all alike."

Ricky has fought — with the solid support of his parents — to be independent, He lives in his own apartment behind his parents' house, He lives up to his nickname of "Mr. Clean" — the former garage with a sign over the door proclaiming it "Ricky's Pad" is spotless.

"Ricky paid for every bit of the renovation with the money he made from Coca-Cola," Mrs. Lamm said. "And I've pushed him. I made him clean up his room and make his bed. Just because he's retarded doesn't mean he gets away with anything. I've put demands on him.

"I've heard parents say, 'He can't do it, he can't.'

"Bull. He can do it. You just have to keep after him. It might take me 100 hours to teach him to tie his shoes, but he can do it."

"Ricky's Pad" is something to see. Ricky has an extensive model railroad collection, but the first thing that grabs your eye is the amazing collection of Coca-Cola paraphernalia everywhere. There are Coca-Cola glasses, bottles, lamps, umbrellas, ashtrays from Paris, mirrors, a kitchen cannister set, calendars, coolers, a working telephone and, yes, Coca-Cola sheets and pillow cases on his bed.

"I love Coca-Cola," Ricky said. "They are No. 1 with me. I don't feel different any more. Now I feel special."

A World Class Eater

You're a big eater, huh?

You're the kind of person who gets the large barbecue dinner? You're the kind of person who pulls two trays through the cafeteria line? You're the kind of person who can really pack it away?

Well, move over. Make way for Mort Hurst, 34. You're nothing but a nibbler.

To say that Mort Hurst can eat a lot is like saying that the Grand Canyon is a hole in the ground, that Dolly Parton has big wigs and that New York City has some tall buildings.

"I like to eat catfish," Mort said the other day. "This restaurant was having one of those all-you-can eat catfish specials for $7, so I went.

"I told the girl to bring me 10 catfish. She said she couldn't bring me that many; so I said if she couldn't, I'd leave.

"She brought me 10 and I ate them all. Then she came back and asked me if I wanted some more.

"I said yes, I did, but not as many as the first time. I told her to bring nine, and I ate them."

That was not one of Mort's big feeds. That was just supper. For when he sets his mind to some serious eating, you'd better stand aside. And pass the ketchup, please.

Take the 1983 Ayden Collard Festival. Mort had always been a big eater, so he thought he'd turn pro — so to speak — and enter the collard-eating contest. With no competition at home except for his brother Don, Mort felt a need to find out just how good he was at shoving the groceries down his throat.

"Anything I go at, I go at 150 percent," Mort said. "There are a lot of people out there going at it 100 percent. So I went into training to stretch my stomach."

The eating contest would be Saturday. On Wednesday night, Mort polished off 300 boiled shrimp, two bowls of slaw, two baskets of hush puppies, two orders of french fries and two pitchers of iced tea.

"I was going to eat more, but I was with my Aunt Brownie Highsmith, and she was embarrassed," he said.

Thursday night, he drank three chocolate milkshakes and two large glasses of iced tea. He ate five hamburgers and five hotdogs, a large can of pork and beans and two bags of potato chips.

Friday, Mort just snacked.

It was hot in Ayden on Saturday. The temperature was above 100 when Mort walked up to the eating table.

"Now I'm 6-foot-2 and weigh 200 pounds, and there stood a man that looked like Goliath," Mort recalled. "I'm looking up at him. He must have been 6-5 and weighed 280 pounds."

He was looking at the legendary D.A. Rodgers, four-time champion collard eater.

They sat down to eat. Mort jumped off to a fast lead, putting down the first pound of collards in one minute and eight seconds, a record.

"I would have done it faster, but I stopped to put ketchup on them," he said.

On they ate, pound after pound of collards disappearing. Finally the collard-eating experience of D.A. Rodgers won out, and Mort was disqualified.

I'm not going to tell you how it happened. It was not a pretty sight. Suffice it to say that the rules require that each collard that goes down has to stay down.

Mort went out with just under six pounds. Rodgers went on to victory with just over six pounds.

But as momentous as those eats are to contemplate, they are nothing compared to the night in Morehead City when Eatin' Mort Hurst secured his rightful place in the world of big eaters.

His boss had invited the boys down for a free weekend of eating and fishing. Mort never did go fishing, but his knife and fork work will long be remembered. On that night in 1972, brave men sat in awe and small children turned away.

It was the Night of the Prime Rib Massacre.

They started with shrimp cocktails, 13 shrimp to the serving. On and on they came, and when they cleared away the first course, Mort had eaten 11 shrimp cocktails. That is 143 shrimp. The appetizer was over.

Then came the main course, the prime rib. Eatin' Mort Hurst was a man with a mission, and his mission was to eat all the meat there was in the civilized world.

That night, as his friends watched, Mort ate 127 ounces of prime rib. That is almost eight pounds of steak.

And that wasn't all. He also ate five baked potatoes and five bowls of salad. He gulped down five pitchers of iced tea. And he covered most of it with two bottles of ketchup.

"When we got through, the waitress came by and asked if we wanted some dessert. I said I thought I did," Mort said.

"I always did like blueberry pie, so I asked her to bring me one. She said she'd be right back with a piece, and I said: 'I didn't say a piece, I said a pie. And some ice cream.'"

So he ate a blueberry pie with a half-gallon of ice cream on top.

"Then we took a walk out on the pier after supper," Mort said. "My wife wanted an ice cream cone, so I had one, too"

As you might expect, Mort grew up at a well-covered breakfast table. Every morning, his mama used to cook three dozen eggs, two pounds of bacon and sit a loaf of bread on the table for just Mort and Don.

There was the day he ate 37 scrambled eggs and two pounds of bacon by himself, the day he ate the 16 chicken breasts, the day he ate 21 hot dogs (all the way). There was the day he ate six entire barbecued chickens and Don ate five, and they took four home for a midnight snack.

"I don't eat like this all the time, just when there's motive or a challenge," Mort said. "I eat regular meals like everybody else. Like when we have barbecued chicken, I never eat more than two whole chickens."

Salty Tales of a Whaler

Russells Creek

The old man spends his days in a well-kept mobile home by the side of a country road. His eyes are fading, and the bone chill of arthritis makes him wear long underwear and keep the heat up high on a sunny autumn day.

He is the last of his breed, the last of the great whalers who rowed out into the stormy Atlantic in open boats in search of the largest creatures on Earth.

His name is Charlie Rose, and you need look no further for the story of the sea and the hard men who fought her for their lives and livelihoods.

He was born in 1893 in Diamond City, the village that once stood on Cape Lookout before it was abandoned to the Atlantic gales that have washed it from the sand and into the mists of history.

But he and his family did not just watch the history that unfolded during their time; they made it.

His grandfather Joe and his grandmother Sophie came from England. Joe was a pound netter by trade. He brought the skill to America, first to the waters off Long Island, N.Y. He then worked his way south off the New Jersey shore and finally to the fishing village of Stumpy Point, where he had a son named Tillman who followed his father to the sea.

Tillman moved farther south to make his life, down to the Core Banks of Carteret County and he helped settle Diamond City. Tillman was to play his own part in this area's history.

They still tell the story about the greatest shipwreck in these waters. It was so cold and stormy the night of Jan. 11, 1886, that to this day "the night the Chrissie Wright came ashore" is the standard by which all miserable nights are measured. Tillman Rose was part of the Chrissie Wright rescue crew, and he brought back a crewman who had lashed himself to the bowsprit to keep from being washed or blown away.

"One day, it must have been in 1904 or 1905, we were down mending nets at the cape," said Mr. Charlie, as he is known to all. "We heard something roaring over our heads and looked around to see what it was. It was making a real racket.

"We looked up and saw it was an airplane. It landed on the flats, and this man come over to us and asked me and my counsins Danny and Joe if we wanted to take a ride in it.

"We didn't mind a bit, but when she hit those air pockets, it was a little rough, don't you know?

"It didn't look like that little engine could do anything, but when we got up and looked down at the cape and the lighthouse and the houses, it was a wonderful-looking thing."

The pilot? Well, his name was Wilbur Wright, and he and his brother had invented the airplane a year or so before, making Mr. Charlie probably the first North Carolinian to ever fly in one.

It was March 16, 1916. Mr. Charlie was at Cape Lookout harbor shooting loons when the cry went out. A whale had been spotted in the shallows, and the whalers rushed to their boats.

Mr. Charlie took the helm of the gas boat that pulled the whale boat as near the whale as possible. His uncle, John Rose, was in the bow of the 22-foot double-ended whaler with a 75-pound harpoon gun to shoulder. His father, Tillman, was in the stern guiding the boat while four men pulled on the oars.

"We fought her for eight hours," Mr. Charlie said. "We hemmed her up in the shallows and finally captured her.

"She measured 12 feet high, 11 feet wide and 57 feet long. Her tail was 16 feet from tip to tip.

"We pulled her up on the beach and used a block and tackle to open her mouth, and I walked in her just like walking in a door.

"You want to know what we got for her? Well, we got 30 barrels of oil from her and three barrels from her jaw and five barrels from her liver. We sold it for $33,000. I cut 365 bones out of her mouth, one for every day of the year.

"This was whaling country in those days. We didn't kill many but look what we got when we did kill one. You got $1.05 a gallon for whale oil then, and that wasn't too bad, I don't think."

Mr. Charlie left the Core Banks when he was 50 and spent the next 30 years buying and selling fish. He became a familiar sight on the Carteret back roads with his pickup loaded with fresh fish.

But he and his family still were making history, this time as boat builders. The men of Harkers Island have long been known for the fine boats they designed and built, and two of Mr. Charlie's nephews were the best of all at the trade.

"I was living on Harkers Island, and my nephews James and Earl decided they'd build themselves a boat," Mr. Charlie said. "They went and helped Brady Lewis build one and then started their own.

"The first one was 33 feet long and 8 wide, and it was the prettiest boat ever built on Harkers Island. They built it for themselves, but somebody came along and wanted to buy it, so they sold it."

So began the famous Rose Brothers boat builders of Harkers Island, the men credited with building the best fishing boats on the Atlantic Coast.

Mr. Charlie served in the Lifesaving Service at Cape Lookout in the Army during World War I and in the Coast Guard during World War II.

He is warm and safe now, miles from the water that was his home for so long, but the seaman beneath the shock of white hair and behind the clouded eyes is still young and strong.

"If I could live on Cape Lookout again, I wouldn't be here more than three seconds longer than it took to pack my stuff," he said.

Secrets and a Deathbed Promise

Asheboro

Bill never understood why his family moved so often, sometimes every two or three months.

"Sometimes we'd move in the middle of the night," Bill said. "I can remember my daddy and mama putting me in a red coaster wagon and pulling me down the road to another mill village.

"We'd leave a house full of furniture, just taking a few clothes with us."

There were other things Bill didn't understand, such as why he had no relatives on his father's side and why, when he visited his father's hometown, he found no one there with his last name.

And he couldn't understand why his father was so nervous every time he was around a police officer.

It wasn't until his father was dying and the 82-year-old man called Bill to his bedside that it all came out.

"Tell them I wasn't so bad," his father said. "Tell them the kind of man you knew me as."

"It hurt my heart," Bill said. "I found out that my father wasn't who I thought he was, that I wasn't who I thought I was. It was a bitter pill to swallow."

For more than half a century, Bill's father had lived on the run, a fugitive from chain gang justice.

Bill knew his father as Lonnie William Rose, but on that cold night in January, he learned the truth.

His father's name was really Thomas Arthur Wise. He wasn't from Germantown, Texas; he was from Cullman, Ala. He was an escaped convict.

It took until 1982 for Bill to piece the story together:

One Sunday morning in 1915, Thomas Arthur Wise, 23, woke up from a Saturday night of drinking in the saloons of Cullman to find a woman by his side wearing a cheap wedding ring and claiming that they had gotten married the night before.

"Daddy did the right thing and went about trying to make a life for them," Bill said. "He worked driving an ice and coal wagon.

"One day he left a $5 bill lying on a table for her to pay the rent. He came home and the money was gone, and he asked her if she'd paid the rent. She said she'd given the money to her brother."

Angered, Thomas Wise went in search of his brother-in-law to get his money back. He found him and a fight broke out. A crowd gathered, most of them friends and neighbors of the brother-in-law.

"Daddy whipped him and took his $5 back," Bill said. "Then the crowd grabbed Daddy and held him while the other man beat him unconscious."

Wise woke up in jail, charged with stealing $5 and a $6 watch. He maintained on his deathbed that he had been framed, that the watch had been planted and that the money was his.

Freed on bail, Wise hopped a freight train, again taking up the life of a hobo that he had lived since he was 9. He was free untill 1916, when he was caught.

He was sentenced to 10 years at hard labor in an Alabama prison. He was in prison for three years.

"There was a fire in the prison, and they moved everyone out, and 500 of them hit the bushes and escaped," Bill said. "Daddy was one of them."

Wise changed his name to Lonnie William Rose and spent the next 55 years running from the law for a crime he swore he never committed.

"One time during the war, Daddy was working in a mill and they said that everyone who worked there had to be fingerprinted since it was a defense plant," Bill said. "Daddy claimed he was in bad health and quit to go work on a farm, but he looked fine to me.

"I used to ask him why we moved so much, why he quit the job at the mill, why we never had any relatives like other people did. He always said, 'Someday you'll understand, son.' "

The family lived all over the South. His daddy was an expert loom repairman, and he never had any trouble getting jobs in textile mills. There were stays in Franklinville and in Woodruff, S.C. They lived in shacks, in millhouses, wherever they could find a home and place where people didn't ask too many questions.

It was while the family was in Franklinville, near Asheboro, in 1923 that Bill was born. He was named Warren William Rose.

"Daddy loved Franklinville and we kept coming back here," Bill said. "He seemed to find peace here."

But the old man kept his secret. He never went back to Alabama, he never saw his parents again, and he never told who he was and what had happened.

"I think part of it was he had a wanderlust in him," Bill said. "I don't think every time we moved was because he thought they were after him again. I think he got used to it and kept moving.

"In 1947, after 28 years on the run, the old man settled in Franklinville and stayed there until he died in 1974.

"On his deathbed, he made me promise that I would get word back to the authorities in Alabama where he was, that I would tell his people in Alabama that he wasn't a bad man, that I would find his parents' graves and put a tombstone on them, and that I would change my name back to what it used to be." "It hurt my heart all to pieces," Bill said. "I had to squall standing right there. Why hadn't he told me before?"

For eight years, Bill Rose kept the pain inside him. Finally, he worked it all out and last summer began to keep the promises made to his dying father.

"I took care of the first promise as soon as Daddy died," he said. "I called the prison authorities in Alabama and asked them if they were still looking for Thomas Arthur Wise.

"They called me back and said that of the 500 men who had escaped with Daddy in the prison fire, 280 of them were still unaccounted for and that Daddy was one of them. I told them they could stop looking, that he was dead.

"I talked to my wife about the other things I'd promised him, and she told me I ought to drop it, just let it die. But in 1982, I had to keep my promises."

He began by getting a telephone book from Cullman and started calling every family named Wise.

"It all happened in 1916, so most of the people who knew Daddy were dead," he said. "I got a story in the Cullman paper that told Daddy's story and what kind of man he was. I told them how he was a good man, a hard-working man who never did one thing wrong for the rest of his life.

"I told them how, when he worked at a movie theater, he used to give those sad-eyed kids sitting on the curb enough money to go to the movies. I told them the kind of man I knew him as."

Two of the promises had been kept, but there were two more.

"I called the city cemetery and asked them if they had graves of my grandparents," Bill said. "All they had was a record that my grandmother had bought a plot but no record of who was buried there, if anybody. There was no marker on the plot.

"They went out with long metal rods and stuck them in the ground until they located the graves of two adults and one child in that plot. The child was my father's little sister, who died young."

Bill went to Cullman and spent a week visiting the few distant relatives he could find, telling them who he was and telling them what had happened to the family legend of the black sheep who had disappeared. Also, before he left, he had markers placed on the graves of his grandparents.

There was one more promise left to keep. For all his life he had been known as Bill Rose, a country music picker who ran away at 14 and spent five years on the honky-tonk trail with Hank Williams before settling down to work in factories and mills around Asheboro.

But his Daddy had asked him to change his name, from Rose to what it should have been, Warren William Wise, a descendant of German Jews who immigrated to Alabama more than a century ago.

"That part of it didn't bother me," the newly named Bill Wise said. "I wanted to be who I really was, and that was the son of Thomas Arthur Wise."

The search and the pain is over. The truth has been told, the promises kept.

"I'm at peace now," Bill Wise said. 'I haven't had a drink in two years, and I feel good about it.

"I just wanted to let people know that my Daddy wasn't a bad man."

There is one more thing. The woman who was beside Thomas Aurthur Wise when he awoke with a hangover that Sunday morning in 1915, the woman who claimed he had married her the night before, the woman who caused the fight that sent him to prison and made him spend his life on the run, living in the shadows, was lying.

They never were married. None of it — the moving in the middle of the night to stay one step ahead of the law, the changing of his name, the lie he lived all his life, the fear — need ever have hapened.

Dog Survives With Food — and Love

He was lying under a bush beside the still waters of a pond, seeking a cool place to die in the searing August heat.

No one knew the dog's name, so he was called Moses because he was found in the bullrushes.

He was about 2, a mixed Irish setter and golden retriever. He wore no collar or tags, and looked as if he had been on his own for six to eight months, eating what he could find and sleeping where he stopped for the night.

He was so starved you could see every bone in his body. Mange had destroyed his once-beautiful coat. His body contained every parasite imaginable, including heartworms. He seemed to have no spirit, no heart for the fight that was to come.

He should have been dead, but the man who found him, Raleigh attorney D. James Jones Jr., decided Moses would not die — not until everything that could be done had been done.

Jones brought Moses to the Wake County SPCA shelter on U.S. 70 in Garner and gave him to shelter manager Peggy Warfle.

"I didn't think he'd make it to the pen," she said. "If the decision had been mine, I would have had him put to sleep then. He had a terrible fight ahead of him and nothing to fight with. There was more wrong than right with him."

Jones would not hear of it. He told Peggy to do everything possible to save Moses and said he would pick up the bill. For six months Peggy often wavered in her determination. Often she thought Moses would, and should die, but not Jones.

"Jim just kept saying, 'But Peggy, he's such a nice dog,' " Peggy said, "And I kept trying to prepare Jim for the possibility of euthanasia. I just didn't think he'd make it."

So the battle for Moses' life was begun.

Peggy decided to treat the mange first while they battled to add weight to the dog. But Moses kept losing weight no matter how much he was fed. He was being washed and dipped daily, and after five weeks his coat was better, but he was no healthier.

Veterinarians decided the heartworm treatment must begin even though it might kill Moses because of his weakened condition. Heartworms are killed with injections of poison, and the treatment can kill dogs much healthier than Moses.

Less than a week after the first injections, Moses stopped eating and was running a high fever. It was pneumonia, and once again everyone expected Moses to die. It was getting late in the year, and cold weather makes fighting pneumonia harder.

Moses could not stand up any more. He lay in his cage at the animal shelter and gasped for breath. The staff kept pumping the medicine into him.

"The look in his eyes would kill you," Peggy said. "He looked like he wanted to die. We had to stand him up to get him to move at all.

"On warm days we'd take him outside and lay him on a blanket. He seemed to enjoy that. But it was getting hard to see him in that condiiton day after day without getting any better. The thought crossed my mind that the easiest thing would be to give him a shot and tell Jim he'd died. But I had given my word.

"The last thing we did every night was check Moses, and he was the first thing we'd check every morning."

Moses got worse. The pneumonia was checked, but by Christmas he began to hemmorhage. Time after time the staff had to take him to veterinarians for blood transfusions.

He seemed to get a little better in early January, but he had not gained weight. Moses weighed about 30 pounds, less than half his normal body weight.

"He acted like he'd finally lost the will to live," Peggy said. "We'd put food in his mouth, and he wouldn't swallow it."

Back to the veterinarians they went, this time for intravenous injections to keep fluids in the poor dog's body. Peggy called Jim again and told him this was it; Moses was dying. He had lost all desire to live. He would not eat.

But there was one slim chance left. Get some food with a sharp smell that perhaps would stimulate his appetite. So Jim showed up at the shelter with a big bag of Vienna sausages, sardines and cat food.

And that was the beginning of the end of the story.

Moses began eating, slowly at first but then more and more as the days went by. A spark came back to his eyes; he began to get up by himself and seemed to want to go outside.

"It was wonderful," Peggy said. "He got to where he'd guard his food dish and he'd snap at you if you went to touch it.

"The old boy was finally acting like a dog."

That's the end of the story. Moses started putting on weight and eating the place out of house and home.

Finally in early February, Fuquay-Varina police officer Mike McDermott came into the animal shelter looking for a dog. And Moses was ready to be adopted.

"Watching that dog ride off to a new home, sitting in the front seat of that pickup truck, was really special to see for all of us," Peggy said. "Of all the dogs I've seen come in here, he was the one I never thought would make it.

"I'm glad we did it."

And Moses.

"He's fine," McDermott said. "He still likes to roam, but he comes home to eat.

"He's a survivor."

The Story of Millie-Christine

Welches Creek

She spoke seven languages, appeared in command performances before the kings and queens of Europe and sang and danced for tens of thousands of wide-eyed customers. She was kidnapped twice, and she was called a freak.

Her name was Millie-Christine McCoy, and she always said she was just one person — one person with two heads, four arms and four legs.

But most people thought and spoke of her as two people, Siamese twins joined at the lower spine. Millie-Christine are the only Siamese twins on record born in North Carolina who were not separated and who survived to old age.

Millie-Christine, born in 1851 in the Columbus County community of Welches Creek, spent 61 years together. Born into slavery and sold to promoters, they grew to captivate the world with their charm and talent.

Millie-Christine were the eighth and ninth children born to Jacob and Monemia McCoy (seven more would follow, all of them "normal"), slaves belonging to Columbus County farmer Jabez McCoy.

Jabez McCoy sold the twins for $1,000, plus 25 percent of any receipts from showing them, to John C. Purvis. How many times they were sold is not known, but by the time they were 10 they were the property of J. P. Smith of Wadesboro, who exhibited them.

They were first kidnapped in New Orleans and taken to England, where they were exhibited. Smith and their mother eventually found Millie-Christine and brought them back to North Carolina. The twins were hidden during the Civil War, but after the war they embarked on a successful show business career.

They sang and danced and talked to the audience — always as one person, saying, "I," not "we." Their audiences included Queen Victoria, who gave them matching brooches, and Edward, Prince of Wales.

They spent much of the money from their performances buying the land on which they had been born.

They retired in 1880 and moved into a 10-room house on the old McCoy plantation property. That house was destroyed by fire in 1909, and they built another smaller house nearby.

Millie-Christine were through with show business, except for occasional appearances at local fairs, but they often welcomed visitors to their home in Columbus County.

Much of the money they made was donated to various causes in the county, including a school for black children.

Millie developed tuberculosis, and the sisters spent several months in a sanitarium in an effort to cure her. But on Oct. 8, 1912, she died.

That left Christine alone but still attached to her dead sister. Doctors, including experts from medical colleges, said the two could not be separated even though Christine was in perfect health.

Christine lay in bed and prayed that her own death would come quickly. She spent the next 17 hours singing hymns until she died.

They were buried near their home, but in the late 1960s their remains were moved to Welches Creek Cemetery east of Whiteville.

The epitaph for the two talented and gracious women, who lived a difficult life as well as it could be lived, reads: "A soul with two thoughts. Two hearts that beat as one."

Lloyd Inman was in the fourth grade when he figured it out.

"It was the most amazing thing," he said. "The teacher showed us a picture of two ladies joined together, and I went home and told my mother about it.

"She said they were the two ladies she'd been telling me about, my aunts.

"She had a picture of them, and I took it to school the next day. I was so full of pride. What made me not feel ashamed over having Siamese twins in my family was that Mother spoke of them as being so proud and polished. When Mother spoke of Mille-Christine, it was almost as if she was sacred in the family."

"In all of her writings she says, 'I'm one,' " Lloyd said, trying to clear up the confusion I felt when trying to figure out how many people we were talking about.

"She said that when God made her, he gave her two heads and two brains because her responsibility was so great. If she considered herself one, I must as well.

"If Christine was speaking, it was always 'Millie-Christine.' If Millie was speaking, it was 'Christine-Millie.' One always put the other one first.

"Millie was more quiet and shy., She liked to crochet and do embroidery. She also did all the decorating for the 10-room Victorian house they built as a retirement home. And Christine let her pick out the jewelry.

"Christine was more a reader. She could recite something after reading it one time, and she loved Shakespeare. And Christine was more willing to allow men to talk to her. Millie didn't.

"They were amazingly close. If Christine was talking to you, Millie could be talking to someone else and then pick up the conversation Christine was having in mid-sentence. Often, they spoke in unison.

"They sensed each other's moods and feelings perfectly and were devoted to each other."

Millie and Christine were joined at the buttocks, but they could not have been separated even with modern medical technology. Christine possibly would have lived but Millie, whose body was incomplete, would have died.

"They were born back to back," said Inman, who is writing a book on the twins. "But as they got older, they got to the place where they could kiss each other on the cheek near the ear. But allthough they were never apart, they never were able to look at each other face to face.

"Nowhere have I ever found that they argued. Their sister Clara, who was their seamstress and traveling companion, kept a detailed diary and she never mentioned that 'Sister,' as she called her, ever argued.

"When they boarded a train, they bought one ticket and when they ordered a meal they got two plates but one check."

The adventures of Millie-Christine, which are often heroic, sometimes tragic, and occasionally funny are best left for another time. Some of those I skimmed over, but the kind of person Millie-Christine turned out to be is inspiring.

"Millie-Christine came home to Columbus County in 1892 to retire," Inman said. "She had half a million dollars in cash, not counting all her jewels and furniture. She bought the plantation where she and her family had been slaves and built a fine house.

"But she also took care of her entire family and built them all houses on the plantation.

"White folks treated her like an exception, not as a black woman in the South was treated then. She got the finest rooms in hotels. She did a lot to bring blacks and whites together because she was someone everyone — black, white or Indian — in Columbus County could be proud of. She was also one of the richest people in the county.

"She built a church and a school for black children and gave money to Shaw University in Raleigh, Bennett College in Greensboro, Johnson C. Smith College, Henderson Institute and Palmer Institute. But she never got, or wanted, credit for it. Every spring a gentleman would come to Palmer Institute with money and leave it. They never knew where it came from.

"She lived a life for the betterment of her people. She was more than just a circus freak, she was a talented, generous black woman who was one of the greatest black women of her time. How many other black women had half a million dollars back then and did with it what she did?"

Psalm 139, verses 13 and 14, were favorites of Millie-Christine, and of Lloyd Inman, the great-great nephew who keeps the memory alive:

"For thou has possessed my reins: thou has covered me in my mother's womb. I will praise thee; for I am fearfully and wonderfully made: marvelous are thy works; and that my soul knoweth right well."

The Happy Life of a Revenooer

The woman told the judge that Garland Bunting sat down at her kitchen table and ate an entire five-layer cake and washed it down with an R.C. Cola. She said that was dessert after he'd polished off the ribs out of a 100-pound hog.

And then he rared back and said, "Ain't y'all got nothing to drink around here?"

Yes, she had something to drink, a little taste of moonshine whisky — and that's what got her in trouble because Garland Bunting was an undercover cop investigating bootleggers.

"To tell the truth, I didn't eat all of the ribs," he said. "But I sure put a dent in 'em."

Meet Garland Bunting, dedicated coon hunter, serious consumer of groceries ("I don't eat nothing but meat and groceries"), guitar player, story teller, buck dancer, scripture quoter and one of the finest undercover agents in the history of the federal Bureau of Alcohol, Tobacco and Firearms.

The ATF has awarded its Gallatin Medal only twice to peole outside the agency. Bunting, the ABC officer for Halifax County, received his last month. It honors 22 years of cooperation with the agency, most of that as an undercover agent.

Bunting's specialty is getting bootleggers to sell him illegal whiskey. To do that he has done everything from running a fish route to working in a sawmill.

"If you go in those places trying to buy whisky and you look like an agent you're going to get killed," he said. "But in 22 years I've never run hot (been identified) by anyone. You've got to talk like a bootlegger and look like a bootlegger. People tell me I ought to have been a salesman because if you can sell a man to the federal penitentiary you can sell anything."

There was one time when Bunting was identified as an undercover agent and a double-barrel shotgun was pointed at him by a man he described as "mean as a yellow dog." But within an hour, this smooth-talking country boy had the bootlegger offering to take him around the country to tell all the other bootleggers to ignore what they'd heard, they could trust this old boy.

Bunting has proved his worth as a salesman, particularly a fish salesman.

"I got me a car and built me a box on the back," he said. "I'd fill it up with fish and go all over the country.

"I knew where the bootleggers were and I had a regular route. I'd pull up somewhere and get up on top of that box and start playing my guitar and harmonica and go to buck dancing.

"I had a litte song that went, 'Put up the dishpan, here comes the fish man. I got catfish, carp and eel, the more you eat the better you feel. I ain't got but a few left, if you don't buy them I'll eat 'em myself.'

"That would draw a crowd and loosen them up, and I'd sell them fish if they had the money and trade fish for moonshine if they didn't have money."

That little scam soon made Bunting a community institution. Before long all the bootleggers trusted him.

"Most of them thought I was a bootlegger, too," he said. "The day the arrests were made (153 of them), one of the women saw me at the police station and said, 'Lawd, if they's got the fish man they's got us all.'

"To tell the truth, that was a lot of fun but I do feel sorry for the next man who goes in there to really sell fish."

Bunting's career in law enforcement began in his home town of Oak City back when the little town was the Saturday night place for loggers and sawmill crews to come and raise a little hell.

"I used to work with the town policeman when he needed me and I took the job on weekends when he got beat up real bad.

"Oak City was tough in those days. I had my clothes torn off me ... and they were women. I worked in a sawmill all week and was a policeman on weekends. I had to win when I went into something. I had no backup, no way to call for help. I had to handle a situation or be handled. It was survival."

The Army made Bunting a military police officer when he was drafted, and it was in Germany when he first learned that he was good at working undercover. He spent much of his two years working on black market cases.

State ABC officials heard about this good old country boy who could fool anybody. After he went back to Oak City they came to him and asked him to work with them. Soon he became an ABC officer.

"I've always cooperated closely with the ATF," he said. "I am a full-time ABC officer for Halifax County but I've worked undercover all over the state when the ATF needed someone to go in and buy whiskey.

"The ATF is one of the most efficient agencies I've ever seen. If it wasn't for them, we couldn't have fought the bootleggers like we have."

Bunting estimates there has been a 75 percent reduction in the amount of moonshine whiskey made and sold in North Carolina in the past 30 years, but it hasn't been stopped. He helped find and destroy two stills in one day last month and is working on finding several others.

"Catching a bootlegger is a challenge beyond anything you can imagine," he said. "They're smart.

"I've spent up to two weeks at a time behind one pine tree watching peons work a still and waiting for the big shots to show up, but I can say there isn't a man walking who has enjoyed their life more than I have."

On the Road

Chapel Hill

Consider for a moment the jalapeno.

It is a simple growth, 2 to 3 inches long, slimy looking and dull green.

It does not look impressive.

Do not be deceived. An atomic bomb doesn't look impressive, either.

There is enough fiery potency hiding beneath a jalapeno's calm exterior to propel a super-stock dragster.

The juice from a jalapeno pepper will burn your skin; it does not have to get into your mouth to work its evil. A bowl of jalapenos on a table will make your eyes water from three feet away.

I do not wish to belabor the point. But to fully understand what happened in Chapel Hill you have to appreciate jalapeno peppers.

It was a sunny Saturday in the parking lot of Tijuana Fats Mexican restaurant and time for the Great Jalapeno Eating Contest.

Forty people had signed up to eat peppers, with $100 going to the person who could eat the most in two minutes. There were two kegs of free beer and much bravado about.

Shoot, how hard would it be to down a bunch of little old peppers? You wait, I'll eat a bunch of them, the contestants bragged.

That was before state Sen. Charles E. Vickery, D-Orange, the master of ceremonies, called them onto stage and positioned them in front of a plate heaped with a bunch of those little old peppers.

Vickery, it must be reported, did not eat a single pepper.

There were two basic styles of pepper-eating. The cautious began by taking a small bite. The silly began by taking whole peppers in their mouths and chomping down.

The result was the same, regardless of style. The first reaction was a distinct widening of the eyes as the awful truth sank in. What have I done?

Some stopped with one pepper. Those were the smart ones. A hundred bucks was not enough. Some hung on and ate perhaps a dozen before throwing up their hands and calling it quits.

There were maybe 12 truly insane people there, people fueled with enough free beer or intense competitive spirit to ignore the pain, to ignore the sweat that popped out on their red faces, to ignore the tears that streamed from their frightened eyes and to keep eating.

The truly great jalapeno eaters ate 20 to 30 peppers during the longest two minutes they ever lived.

Then there was Jack Jackson of Charlotte, a junior at Carolina. Jackson ate 36 peppers, and when it was over, he said: "I don't know why I did it, but I'll never do it again. It is insane."

And J.J., as he is known to his friends, was prepared.

"I called some doctors in Charlotte and they all told me if I was going to do something this stupid to drink Maalox before and afterward. Then I got a dentist to prescribe some Xylocaine (which dentists use to make patients' mouths numb) for me.

"My mouth never burned. They were easy going down. Now I am dying."

I will try to be delicate. J..J. and I were talking while a friend helped him stand as straight as he could stand, which was about half-mast. I noticed his eyes did not seem to be focusing too well, and he had a distant look about him.

I was at midquestion when he abruptly broke off our conversation to rush across the street, where he appeared to carry on a conversation with his shoe tops for a bit. He came back looking much better.

"I am 23," J. J.said, "and still dumb after all these years."

Clark Church, the mild-mannered owner of Tijuana Fats, said later: "This was kind of barbaric, but it was fun. We had six cases of pepper ready. But they only ate a case and a half.''

Perhaps the reason all the peppers were not eaten was best summed up by a contestant who consumed but one pepper. When it was over, he said, ''I talked to God while I ate the first one and God told me to quit.''

Then I decided that to properly report on this event, I had to eat a jalapeno. I took one small bite, perhaps a quarter-inch piece.

God talked to me, too, and he told me the same thing. God, as usual, was right.

A Town's Time to Remember

Morehead City

I wish you could have been there.

You could have seen the smiles for yourself, you could have felt the lump in your own throat, you would have blinked away the tears in your own eyes, and I wouldn't be left with paltry black words on white paper to tell you what is was like.

Everybody said the same thing: It was wonderful. They felt lucky to be a part of it.

The stars of the day were 69 young men and women from the Caswell Center in Kinston, a home and treatment center for retarded young people.

With 30 Caswell staff members, they had come to Morehead City for their sixth annual overnight trip.

''The Jaycees get all the credit, but we don't deserve it,'' Morehead City Jaycee President Dobey Burroughs said. ''The people of Morehead City do this. All we have to do is tell 'em the kids are coming, and everyone wants to help. We have to turn people down who want to do something for them.''

What the people of Morehead City do is love the kids at Caswell. Restaurants like Sanitary Seafood Restaurant, Capt. Bill's and McDonald's open their doors to the kids, most of them severely to profoundly retarded, many in wheelchairs, and feed them like kings.

The Holiday Inn at Atlantic Beach sets aside 50 rooms; the Kentucky Fried Chicken restaurant gives them lunch. The Dairy Queen takes care of desseert. They're taken on a two-hour boat trip aboard the Carolina Princess. And it doesn't cost anyone a dime.

"The people of Morehead City feel like they own these kids, and many of these kids have never belonged to anyone, even their own families," Caswell staff member Val Carmine said, "Can you imagine how good it makes the kids feel to belong to someone?"

Yes, I can imagine. When Capt. Jimmy "Woo-Woo" Harker started the engines on the 65-foot Carolina Princess, there was a cheer and applause. Eyes that for the rest of the year see little more than the walls of an institution shone as they felt the sting of the sea breeze, danced when the other boaters they met waved at them, thrilled when the crew from the Fort Macon Coast Guard Station put on a show with the fireboat in the harbor.

"You know, everybody has problems, but when you see these kids you know you don't have any worries at all," Harker said. "I wouldn't miss it."

Susan Kenney, Holiday Inn reservations manager, said, "These kids deserve a chance to come to the beach like anyone else. They are happy to be here, and we love having them. Actually, we look forward to it. It is a pleasure to see the joy it brings them.

"These kids are so well-behaved and well-chaperoned that we have less problems with them than we would with 50 rooms of teenagers here for a prom wekend. They'll always be welcome."

Boat rides and fish dinners are fine, but these are young people and for them the highlight is the annual luncheon dance. This year the band was the Detroit Wheels from Virginia Beach. The band members weren't too sure what to expect. All they knew was that to get the job playing at the motel for a week they had to agree to play this lunchtime gig for nothing.

They soon learned what was going on. The first blast of music brought those who could to the dance floor in a cheering burst of energy.

You could see the grins on the musicians' faces from the back of the room.

People danced alone, with each other and with people in wheelchairs. Sex and race didn't matter. Insurance executives boogied with people for whom brushing their teeth and tying their shoes are lifetime accomplishments. Denise Hauser, first mate on the morning cruise, never did sit down. And they all had goofy-looking smiles on their faces.

"I couldn't believe it," guitarist Don Whitley said. "That was from the heart. They'll remember this for the rest of their lives. I was close to tears most of the time."

He wasn't alone. People danced and wiped their eyes. People cheered like crazy when two young men got up and sang with the band. Hotel staffers danced and clapped. Strangers who wandered in danced. It was an hour of unbridled joy and grins to light up the darkness of lives lived in the shadows.

The joy reached every person in the room. It touched them in that deep part of their souls where all of us are equals.

"This is the only night each year that many of these kids get to spend outside Caswell," Val Carmine said. "For them this is the highlight of their year. They'll talk about it and wait for it for a whole year."

So will the people of Morehead City.

I wish you could have been there.

Tradition at a Backwoods Bash

"This," Rusty Walker said quite modestly as things were drawing to a raucous close, "is the redneck social event of the season."

Raleigh may have the Debutante Ball, Rocky Mount may have the Spring German and Morehead City may have its Sandbar Party, but the boys at Harrells Store have the Black River Breakdown.

And it is some kind of party.

This was the third year of the now-traditional Labor Day weekend blowout, and by the time the night was over upwards of 800 country boys had guzzled a lot of beer, danced in the dust for five hours with their country girls, whooped and hollered and waved their cowboy hats and partied with the top two country bands in the state.

This was not some commercial enterprise or official civic functional. The Super Grit Cowboy Band and the Bill Lyerly Band played for expense money only. There was no admission charge and no advertising. The only way you knew it was happening was if someone told you about it and if someone told you that you were welcome.

But this is more than a story about a good party. It is a story about loyalty.

"It all got started back in 1975," said Charlie Marshburn, one of the organizers. "About 10 of us had grown up here together and we're still hanging around together, and we like any kind of music, as long as it's country.

"We heard about this band called Super Grit, and we started following them. We'd go everywhere they played — from Raleigh to the beach."

Joe Jones, another party conspirator, said: "We don't have no sports in Harrells, and no hobbies. What we'd do on weekends is go listen to the bands and we always asked them to play a song for the boys from Harrells Store."

Harrels Store is what Harrells used to be known as before it changed from a community to a town, and lots of folks still call it that.

Billy Lyerly, a former member of Super Grit and now leader of his own band, said: "When you're just starting out, you beat your head against a lot of walls trying to get people to listen to your kind of music. These boys were the first to pick up on what we were doing and we owe them a lot.

"Country is big now, but they were there with us in the beginning. And if it all ends tomorrow, they'll still be with us. The least we can do is come down here and play for them.

Clyde Mattocks, leader of Super Grit, echoed Lyerly's feeling: "This is a tradition for us. These are our hard-core fans. . . . This is our party as much as theirs.

"It's people like this who keep the music going. All this really is an extension of back-porch picking, and that's always the most fun."

Ten friends chipped in money to get the Labor Day bash started. In three years, they've managed to get a permanent stage built and power lines run into the yard of the ramshackle hunting cabin in the woods they call the Foxhole, a private place they've been going to for years.

For the last two years they've taken a donation from the crowd to help with expenses for the bands, and every year they've lost money.

"This is wht we do all winter, sit around and plan for the Breakdown," Marshburn said. "It costs us money, but it's worth it."

The crowd started gathering by 3 p.m. At 5 o'clock an inner group of 200 or so were invited over to Wlker's house to devour two pigs. The music cranked up at 7:30.

From then until 12:30 a.m., it was full-tilt party time. Lyerly's band kicked it off under a clear sky and a shining half-moon, but he was only into his third song when Mattocks, a snake-smooth steel guitar player, joined him. From then on it was a giant jam session.

Bands formed and reformed as the night moved on, doing everything from the old Hank Williams and Bob Wills standards to the new songs that both bands have recorded recently.

When you've stood in the deep woods on a starry night and listened to the lonesome sound of bluesman Danny Joe Reagan singing "I'm So Lonesome I Could Cry," backed up by the best bands in North Carolina, at a party put on and attended by a group of people who like each other and the music, you can begin to feel the magic of country music.

It's like Joe Jones said as the bands closed with a bouncing, hand-clapping medley of "I Saw The Light" and "Will the Circle Be Unbroken":

"It don't get no better than this."

It's a General Store Tradition

Spring Hope

Fellows, we've been doing it all wrong.

It must have been Clark Gable in "Gone With the Wind" who taught us down-home swains that to get the Southern girl of your dreams you have to be devastatingly suave.

Boy, was he wrong.

For all his cool, Rhett Butler ended up with the obnoxious Scarlet O'Hara. J.R. "Cotton" Hildreth, on the other hand, won a terrific Southern lady by telling her he was bald-headed, flat-footed and bow-legged and that his name was — are you ready for this? — Jasper Suckfinger.

"Well," Cotton said, "it was all true." Except for the Jasper Suckfinger part.

What was Beth Baker's response?

"Well, come on over here," she told him, "and let's see what you look like."

Cotton knew he had a winner, so he hung up the phone and rushed right over. She was a teacher in Pinehurst, and he was in nearby Southern Pines awhile for some Air Force training. Being a bold and decisive fighter pilot, he proposed on the first date. Two months later, she accepted.

"I wrote her mother and gave her some references," Cotton said.

"And she checked every one of them out," Beth replied.

Cotton and Beth Hildreth eventually retired to Spring Hope after a life spent in the Air Force. Now they run Sykes Seed Store, the store that Duck Sykes and his daddy ran for 85 years in downtown Spring Hope.

Duck, also known as Johnny, had a general store in Spring Hope that was one of those local attractions people coming home didn't dare miss visiting.

I liked Duck and his dark, jumbled and homey-friendly place.

Duck died a couple of years ago. When I heard that Cotton and Beth had taken over the store, I went back to see what they'd done to it.

They've made it better.

"We didn't want to change the flavor too much," Cotton said. "About all we did was clean it up some."

That must have been a herculean task. Duck had at least one of everything, and it all was jammed onto shelves and into display cases (with broken glass) in a haphazard way that seemed to make perfect sense to Duck alone.

Now the shelves are straight and the glass display cases shine as they did when the store was prosperous. Of course, the button suspenders are still there.

"It's a ratty old store, but it is a Spring Hope landmark," said Cotton, a retired Air Force major general who grew up in Arkansas. "I tried to find someone else to buy it, but they were going to close it down. Beth said we couldn't to that, so we bought it."

Cotton had another reason for buying Sykes Seed Store. An accomplished gardener, he enjoys being around potting soil, seeds and plants, and he knows what he's talking about.

The gardening supplies are the business side of the store. The other side is a little less mercenary.

The store opens every day at 7 a.m. Almost immediately, all the straight-backed chairs that surround the coal stove are filled with the regulars, people like writer Roy Wilder, magistrate Stanley Lamm and the Taylor boys. They do what stove huggers have been doing for centuries: they talk, they tell lies and they solve the world's problems.

"One of the problems is knowing who everyone is," Beth said. "I was gone from here for 25 years, and I've got a lot of family around here.

"One day a man came in and we were talking and I was trying to figure out who he was. You know how you don't want to make them think you don't who they are?

"He asked me, 'Do you know my mother?'

"I said, 'Yes, I know her.'

" 'Well, who is she?' he asked. I don't think he knew."

The folks still stop in at Sykes Seed Store when they come home for visits. Cotton and Beth do a pretty good business in country hams, even mailing some out of state to provide a taste of home for people in the less-cultured parts of this country — places where people look at you funny when you talk about redeye gravy.

There are some things they haven't sold yet, including 25-year-old cans of Bab-O cleanser that have coupons on the back for U.S. Savings Stamps.

"Savings stamps had to be redeemed by 1959," Cotton said.

"We sell it, dust and all," Beth said. "People just blow the dust off and go on."

I wondered how Cotton was fitting in with North Carolina's general store society. Then he told me about how when he was a general in Thailand he held a pig-picking for his troops. Any man who would hold a pig-picking 10,000 miles from Eastern North Carolina has to be part Tar Heel.

"I wouldn't what to be here as long as Duck was," Cotton said. "I wouldn't want to leave the store to go to the hospital to die, but it's fun running this place. You meet a lot of nice people."

Drop by next time you're through Spring Hope. The place isn't really a museum reproduction of how general stores used to be. It just looks that way — brass spittoon, good company and all.

Stay Away From Gaston's Grouches

Lowell

Their mascot is Ebenezer Scrooge. They think that the movie "Pollyanna" should be censored and that "If a man wakes up feeling happy, he should know right then that something is wrong."

"We recommend a cold shower to wipe the smile off your face," says Dock Ayers, president of the Greater Grouches of America, a Society for People Who Were Born in a Bad Mood.

The GGA pledge says it all: "We believe that it is our inherent right to hack off the other person; that society is best served when we are hacking off the other person; and if a society does not want to be hacked off, then SO WHAT!"

In Lowell, a Gaston County town about 20 miles west of Charlotte, the nights are sometimes long, leaving the likes of Ayers and his friends little to do but sit around and complain. Besides, Lowell is a pretty ugly, boring little town. As if that wasn't enough, living so close to Charlotte would put anybody in a rotten mood.

The story probably is made up, but Ayers — an unsavory looking character with Yasser Arafat stubble, a soggy cigar stub and a foul scowl — says the idea for the GGA began when a woman who worked for him brought him a birthday cake.

"Being the grouch that I am, I asked her why she didn't bring the forks and plates, too," he said. "It looks like she would have brought some napkins."

Ayers says that incident got him labeled as a grouch, and when a group of his friends got together and realized they all were grouches, the GGA was born.

"We hold an annual meeting on Dec. 28, because that is right in the middle of those awful holidays, and we think they need to be broken up," he said.

To get things started in the right spirit, the GGA announced its first awards. Ayers was named Grouch of the Year.

White House big-shot Edwin Meese III was named 1983 Humanitarian of the Year for his statement, "I don't know of any authoritative figures that there are hungry children" in America

Joan Rivers was the top vote getter for Miss Congeniality.

Former Ohio State football coach Woody Hayes, who ended his career by punching out a Clemson player, was named Sportsman of the Decade. The 1983 Sportsman of the Year award went to ex-ex-ex-New York Yankees manager Billy Martin.

Mr. T received the award for the Most Pleasing Bad Mouth Attitude of the Year.

From the world of politics, Sen. Jesse A. Helms was voted Politician of the Year. James G. Watt was the only dual winner, sweeping the Toastmaster of the Year and Environmentalist of the Year awards.

Talking to Ayers was not a lot of fun, but I did get him to expand on some of the philosophy and practices of big-time grouchiness.

"We like to put big air horns on our cars to take care of elderly pedestrians," he said.

"The expression 'Have a nice day' is bad enough, but I was in a restaurant the other day and the ticket said 'Have a great day.' A great day? I left the waitress a penny tip.

"We think smiles are extremely depressing, and as a professional photographer, I like to take pictures of crying babies.

"We hate white beards. It makes people think of Santa Claus. The only time we like Santa Claus is when he's giving us something, because we believe it is better to take than to give.

"We tell our members that if they ever get up feeling happy to mark that side of the bed so they'll never get up on that side of the bed again. And if that doesn't work, we have them call another member who tells them every bad thing he can think of until the mood passes.

"We like attack dogs and hate grandmothers because they do our cause a lot of harm.

"The only problem we have had so far is that somebody might think we're serious about this and not realize we're just trying to have some fun."

That, of course, is the whole idea, as was my grouchy description of Ayers and Lowell.

"To me, the funniest thing about all this is that I'm probably the least grouchy person I know," said Ayers, a smiling, friendly man.

You, too, can join the GGA, for yourself or some grouch you know. You can write the GGA at 116 N. Main St., Lowell, N.C. 28098 for more information.

"What we're looking for, besides members, is ideas for our book, '2,000 Different Ways to Hack Off the Other Person.'" Ayers said. "For instance, the best way for a waitress to hack off a customer is to spill just a little bit of coffee into the saucer. That way he get spots on his tie with the first sip."

A Day When Youth Returned

Durham

It was a day they could all be young and whole again.

The old gunfighter was there, dressed in black the way the others remembered him. His still striking face was etched with the mark of good days and bad nights — of pretty ladies who smiled when he was a hero and young toughs who thought they could take him when fame had faded.

But somehow he looked more impressive. The gunfighter had aged with style.

The buckaroos who rode with him 40 years ago watched his every move as he stood in front of them, slowly uncoiling that blacksnake bullwhip. Did he still have it, the old touch that used to send the whip flashing in the sunlight?

Suddenly, the whip streaked like black lightning, straight at them, the tip snapping like a Colt .45. The buckaroos smiled and relaxed.

Yeah, he still had it. He still could take the best of them with a gun or whip, the way he had when they all were a lot younger.

They made themselves more comfortable. Crutches were leaned against the wall, wheelchairs jockeyed for position and battered bodies sought comfort on the hard chairs.

They were there because they also had been gunfighters. But there was a difference. They had done it for real.

The old veterans who crowded into the small, stuffy room on the third floor of the Veterans Administration hospital in Durham didn't seem to mind that Lash LaRue wasn't 8 feet tall, the way he had been on lovely Saturday afternoons when they sat in darkened wonder and watched him ride his black horse across a silver screen.

It was enough that he was there, that he cared enough to come see them, that he remembered them the way they remembered him.

The over-the-hill gang that tamed the West was riding again, hell bent for leather, the smell of gunsmoke and hot lead was in the air.

Somebody passed out popcorn — it was a nice touch — and, as the lights dimmed and the shades were drawn, the clattering projector whirled them on a trip through time, back to the days of their innocence.

The gunfighter's eyes, looking through thick glasses, watched the screen as intently as they did, watching the first appearace of what would become a Hollywood legend.

The movie was called "The Song of Old Wyoming," the first western ever made by Al "Lash" LaRue, the Louisiana kid who always wanted to be a cowboy.

"I walked into producer Bob Tansey's office to get the part," their hero said. "He asked me if I was a good actor. I told him I was the best actor who'd ever been in his office. He told his secretary that I was either a good actor or nuts.

"Then he told me that the part called for me to use a bullwhip. I told him that I'd used a bullwhip all my life.

"I got the part and then went down and rented two bullwhips. I'd never had one in my hands in my life.

"I practically beat myself to death with that whip trying to learn how to use it. Finally I told Bob that I was killing myself with the whip and showed him the scars on my back. He was ready to throw me out of the movie. But he finally hired somebody to teach me how to use it and I took to it like a duck takes to water."

Lash wasn't the star of his first movie. That part went to Eddie Dean, a singing cowboy in a white hat. Lash played The Cheyenne Kid, a hired gun brought to town by evil bankers trying to run out of town a good woman that every body called Ma.

The buckaroos stirred when The Kid rode on the screen. They nodded together when he uncoiled that whip the first time, and they smiled in the dark when he shot a gun out of Ringo's hand.

They knew, as Ma said, "I have a feeling down deep that the The Kid ain't all outlaw."

The first time that Lash LaRue ever popped his whip on the big screen was a dandy. He used his whip to pick a flower for a pretty girl. Boy, was she impressed with that.

One of the greatest death scenes in the Old West brought the movie to an end. Shot down in the dust, The Kid looked up at The Hero and said, "I was always told I'd die with my boots on. I want to fool 'em. Slip my boots off."

And on his tombstone they wrote, "In the worst of us there is some good."

Yeah, Lash fooled 'em all. He made those sick and hurt old buckaroos think they were young again, that it was Saturday afternoon, not Friday, that they weren't in a hospital, that it was the matinee of their lives and not, for many of them, the last act.

And they fooled him, too.

The old gunfighter never looked better than when his gang gathered around him at the end and asked him for autographs. He wasn't old, and they weren't in wheelchairs. The glory had never faded and the wars had never happened.

And you could almost hear, once again, the jingle of a silver spur.

Dream City in Edgecombe County

St. Lewis

It is amazing what you can miss if you don't look closely while you're driving down the road.

Take this little community in Edgecombe County. Now if you whip along N.C. 42 or N.C. 124, the two roads that bypass the town on either side, you won't see much here, just a little sign that proclaims the place was founded in 1850 and from the looks of things, it has been going downhill since.

"You missed the mall, I guess," said Mayor Lee Walston. "And did you see the St. Lewis International Airport?"

Well, no, I didn't. But they were probably over yonder on the other side of the woods, out the back door of Mayor Walston's combination woodworking shop and St. Lewis Town Hall.

"Well, no wonder you didn't see anything, this here is the residential district," the Lord High Mayor said, "Progress is all around us."

Actually, there are two towns called St. Lewis, one the little wide spot in the road that passers-by see; the other a full-blown fantasy town that lives in the fertile imagination of the whimsical make-believe mayor.

"The town fathers needed a good man to be mayor," said Walston, 66 and a lifelong resident of both places called St. Lewis. "They pay me $60,000 a year plus expenses. I run the place, lock, stock and barrel.

"Most of the town's money comes from Mayor's Court that I hold every Monday night. I fine 'em based on how much money they've got and who they live with.

"We have a good export business going here. We have them big Concordes flying in here from Columbia. We send them apple brandy and they send us their exports. Why we've got 1,500 people working in our brandy factory alone.

"We ain't got no crime. We get some of them Saturday night petty offenses and I throw them in jail. They don't get nothing to eat but one slice of cornbread, and that's it. They're real glad to get out. If they get unruly, I shoot 'em with a fire hose. If things get bad, we've got a whipping post.

"Agriculture is big business here. We've developed a strain of strawberries that we crossed with pineapples. We've got 100-pound strawberries that have a hard shell. Makes 'em ship and store better.

"Unemployment isn't a problem in St. Lewis because everybody here works for me. We were getting us a few food stamps before Reagan came in, like $50,000 worth a month, and I gave them to who I wanted to, the ones that took care of me.

"The future looks bright for St Lewis. The Japanese are coming in with an electric airplane plant. The extension cords to operate them will be made of rubber, so if they get in trouble, we'll just snap 'em back to earth.

"We've got us a gunshop coming in here that makes guns that won't shoot but five bullets. After five, it starts throwing brickbats and pop bottles.

"They should work good with the St. Lewis Kennel Club. They've got a birddog there that one time pointed so hard he broke the tailgate out of a pickup truck. What he does is run birds down a hole and puts his paw over the hole and lets 'em out one at a time so you can shoot them."

Being the mayor of such a thriving community is clearly a full-time job, but Mayor Walston finds the hours to put in a little time at the Farmers Warehouse where he is, as he put it, "chief flunky in charge of everything."

He is a good mayor, he says, but then you know how politicians exaggerate things. He claims he took a correspondence course in the fine art of mayoring, and it has been good for St. Lewis and good to him.

"They pay me $60,000, but they put in a few bonuses in every now and then, like eggs and chickens and stuff and, of course, they keep me in plenty of apple brandy," he said.

Plans for the future, while grandiose, are shadowy.

"Of course, we'll have the Olympics soon, and we'll have us a college football stadium," he said. "We plan to build the stadium before we build the college.

"First things first, you know."

Soon it was time to leave. As the skyline of St. Lewis faded in the rearview mirror, I paused for a moment to catch a last glimpse of the thriving metropolis that is the biggest thing between Macclesfield and Temperance Hall. I turned around and looked back.

Lo and behold, it was gone. There was nothing left but the smile on Lee Walston's face and the gleam in his eyes.

You Can't Erase Those Memories

Fayetteville

The last Street Angel had blue tattoos on her thin ankles.

The law says you have to keep moving if you're a topless dancer, even when it's noon and you're trying to eat a bag of potato chips. So she danced along on a recent day, munching and shuffling and thinking about some other place.

Time had run out for the 500 Block of Hay Street, and it was time to move on.

Down the 500 Block where 10 years ago party crowds used to jam a jumping joint called the Town Pump, a graffiti artist had written the finale: "July 28, The Day Hay Street Died."

The politicians are happy. Mayor Bill Hurley had promised that, if elected, he would clean up the 500 Block, but so had every mayor.

The businessmen are happy. John Monaghan of Fayetteville Progress, a non-profit development group, said the strip of bars is worth only $800,000. With the bars gone, he swore that development worth as much $15 million would move onto or near the 500 Block.

But Hurley didn't clean up the 500 Block. And the businessmen didn't clean up the 500 Block, although they convinced the Fayetteville City Council to put up $3 million to buy just the strip of storefronts on the street's south side.

The 500 Block, born in war, died in peace. Like a dinosaur, its time had passed.

They say 800 people gathered the last day, July 28, when it took a wrecking ball seven tries to punch a symbolic little hole in the front of the old Town Pump on the corner.

That many used to gather on the 500 Block on a slow Tuesday the week before an Army payday. One table of fresh-faced paratroopers, away from home for the first time, fueled with cold beer and late adolescent bravado, could have punched the hole a lot quicker.

The 500 Block was Fayetteville, no matter how the straight people protested the image, because Fayetteville is a soldier town, and soldiers spread the fame of the 500 Block to battefields and barracks from Berlin to Khe Sahn.

It never lived up to its billing, but no place could have. The 500 Block was nothing more than a collection of enterprises designed to relieve soldiers of their fear, their fatique, their loneliness and their paychecks. Other merchants in Army towns do the same things; the 500 Block was just more open about it.

There never were more than 19 bars, and that count came in the early 1970s. The bars' names will live in olive drab memories: The Seven Dwarfs, with that gorgeous mural of the Disney characters, the Bunny Club, the Kings Den, the always friendly Pop-A-Top Lounge.

Some people say the Block was born in World War II, but it really made its mark with Vietnam. There still were only two bars on the street by 1966, but war and the warriors had arrived.

Fort Bragg was a busy place, and the 500 Block was busier. The only bus route between the base and downtown started and ended on the Block.

There were big bucks to be made from the young soldiers. They were going off to war, but before they left, they wanted something to remember. The Block gave it to them.

They could get drunk, watch half-naked women dance, eat great meals at a good little place called the Brooklyn Spaghetti House, find companionship from the Street Angels (many of whom were really male transvestites), get a popular tattoo that said "Death Before Dishonor" and, when times got hard just before payday, hock their high school class rings for bus fare and one last beer. They got a lot of laughs and a lot of memories. A few of them also got robbed.

But then came peacetime, and the draftees stopped coming, Professional soldiers with bigger paychecks took their places.

Now the soldiers could afford cars, and they spread out from the Block, out to Bonnie Doone and the maze of trailer parks where the Street Angels moved to ply their historic trade.

The city saw the end coming. The fresh-faced girls who had followed the soldiers were gone, replaced by hard-eyed Korean and Vietnamese matrons who learned their trade in battlefield bars and brothels.

The Block lost its wartime insouciance and became something more sinister.

All of downtown was dying. Suburban shopping malls had bled it dry, and the city began eyeing the 500 Block as more of an opportunity than a money-making strip of lightweight sin and skin. The city turned on the Block like a pack of sharks turn on a wounded member.

Police Chief Danny Dixon went after it with the Street Crimes Unit, putting enough pressure on the hookers to drive them into the county.

They used zoning laws, ABC regulations, city privilege licenses and a lot of money. The 500 Block reeled from the punches.

It isn't over yet. The Block is too tough to die overnight. There's a bar left where you can still pay $20 for a "special" drink for a bargirl and then go upstairs with her and drink it in private.

And a funny thing happened the day the wrecking ball punched the hole in the Town Pump wall, something that will keep the 500 Block of Hay Street alive as long as old soldiers gather to tell war stories.

A few men in the crowd, wearing suits and paunches instead of uniforms and hangovers, picked up a brick or two to take home.

One last time, the 500 Block gave them something to remember it by.

A Satisfactorily Bloody Premiere

Morehead City

I'll tell you what kind of crowd it was.

Pam Cooper was handing out maps on how to get to the party at the Bogue Banks Country Club, but only the out-of-towners took one. Everyone else knew where it was, thank you.

"Everyone who is anyone is Carteret County is here tonight," sniffed one high roller, while ice cubes surrounded by expensive liquor rattled in her plastic cup.

Never have so many sat in such sequined, tuxedoed, bejeweled and furred splendor to see so many close-up and full color beheadings, roaring outboard-motor propellers jammed into bodies and novel and best-undescribed medical procedures performed with a stainless steel fishing gaff.

It was the official world premiere of the first movie made in Atlantic Beach, a little number called "Fall Break," and everyone was so proud of Buddy Cooper, the local boy who wrote, paid a half-million dollars for and directed the film. He even played in the band that recorded the movie's theme song.

Never mind that the movie was made to appeal to the lowbrow, teenage droolers of the world. It was filmed in Carteret Country, had a lot of Carteret County people in it and was the best execuse to dress up in fancy clothes in January that anyone could think of.

Well, maybe not everyone was there. A few people didn't make it, people such as the governor, anyone even remotely associated with the state's growing film industry and the director/writer/producer/musician's own mother.

"She said this was not her kind of movie," said Cooper, an Atlantic Beach attorney.

Then the house lights darkened, the beer cooler that one oh-so-elegant couple had brought was opened and the pop-tops popped (don't snicker, they were the only ones who knew that sneaking beer into this kind of movie was absolutely the correct thing to do), and the mayhem began.

For the next hour and a half, Carteret's finest residents watched a movie that could have been subtitled "Death to the Preppies." In it, four of the most obnoxious collegiates you would ever hope not to meet were drowned, gigged, propellered and gaffed in what Cooper has proudly billed as the world's first horror/slasher/splatter/hamburger flick with a nautical theme.

It was done in brutal color, sickening closeups and terrific special effects and is an obvious drive-in hit. Some in the audience gasped at the mayhem. Some sat with eyes closed and didn't see a thing. And of every four first-nighters who got an unexpected urge to to the bathroom every time the maniac's creepy music started playing, only two returned. A number of us laughed.

The hussy who took off her clothes for a midnight swim was obviously a goner, as was her hunk boyfriend.

Next to go was Ralph the Jerk, followed by his girlfriend, who shamelessly ran around in her see-through nightgown with lights always shining from behind her.

A deputy sheriff was beheaded, and in a moment that will long stand as a monument to hilarious bad taste and in-jokes, a police officer's leg was amputated.

The officer was played by Raleigh attorney John Bode, a Vietnam veteran who lost a leg in the war.

"I loved it," Bode said. "It gave me a real feeling of deja vu."

When it was over, after Buddy had been given a thunderous standing ovation, the audience picked up the hems of its long dresses and brushed the popcorn from its satin lapels and headed for the lobby, where it was met by klieg lights, TV news teams, newspaper photographers and a crowd of second-show low-renters who were lined up to pay to see the homegrown horror movie.

They headed in a well-chromed and polished procession to the country club, where they drank free liquor of all varieties, with the exception that no one ordered a Bloody Mary.

It is a highly moralistic tale that Cooper has delivered, as all of the genre try in their tongue-in-cheek best to do. Lest you think it is nothing more than an evening of mayhem without redeeming social importance, just mega-gore without a message, listen to what one mother said to her 14-year-old daughter as they left the premiere.

"Remember one thing," she said, looking stricken and obviously concerned about the lasting effects the movie might have on Her Precious, although Precious hershelf had a bit part in the movie. "The virgin lived."

My Adventures

When life hands you a lemon, you do not have to, as the wise old sage says, make lemonade.

You can always go back to bed.

Or, as I say, if at first you don't succeed, to heck with it.

I had been looking forward to the day for a long time. Hilda Livingstone, a staffer at the Marine Resources Center on Roanoke Island, had sent me a news release about a whaling expedition on Oct. 17.

The center had chartered a 65-foot boat and was selling seats on the Crystal Dawn, perhaps the finest boat name I've heard lately. We hardy band of sailors were to set sail at 6 a.m. that Saturday and cruise into the Atlantic looking for migrating whales.

How nifty, I thought. I had seen whales in all those Jacques Cousteau specials and they looked neat to me. And the way the Japanese and Russians are killing them off, there may be a time before long when they will be but a memory.

I'll tell you how bad I wanted to see whales, I wanted to see whales so bad that I missed the Carolina-State game — and I had a ticket.

Boy, was I ready to see whales. All week long I walked around saying things like "Thar she blows." I even had a watch cap just like Cousteau's and a military shirt with a turtleneck sweater underneath, sunglasses and a jacket named a "Survivalon." This coat, the tag said, was guaranteed to keep you alive in frigid waters. Actually, what keeps you warm is steaming over how much the darned thing costs.

Planning was intense. I got my binoculars ready and cleaned the lenses. I packed enough food to feed Capt. Ahab and all his crew on the Pequod for days while they searched for Moby Dick. I started taking seasickness pills the day before the cruise. I like to lay down a good base.

Getting up at 4:30 a.m. is never a lot fun, but it wasn't bad that day. I was too excited to sleep anyway. I took more anti-seasick pills and went down to my friend Guy Munger's room to awaken him. That's when I noticed the wind.

Boy, was it a chilly wind coming out of the northeast. The 24-hour weather service informed me the wind was a steady 20 mph. I began to get a tightening in my stomach. Isn't this what these Bankers call a nor'easter, and isn't that bad?

The car swerved a lot as I drove toward the Crystal Dawn. Sure was windy. And cold.

There was no one aboard the Crystal Dawn. It was still dark on board. I felt trouble was in the wind. I took another seasick pill.

Hilda gave me the bad news. Capt. Alan Foreman had said that not only was he not going to take the Crystal Dawn out to sea that day, he didn't even think he could clear Oregon Inlet.

"The wind is blowing 39 miles an hour at Diamond Shoals," he said. "That's too rough."

My macho rebelled for a moment, a very brief moment. Then I thought about it. If an Outer Banks charter skipper says it is too rough, I can imagine how this landlubber would react to the 9- and 10-foot waves that were rippling the horizon. If you don't think that is rough, look at your ceiling. Most ceilings are 8-feet high. Imagine a wave 2 feet higher than that.

Suddenly, the 65-foot boat looked like a dinghy and I felt better about his decision. I also may have been ripped on seasick pills.

So I missed the whales. It did me no good at all to hear that charter captains the day before had seen hundreds of 25-foot pilot whales and dozens of 100-foot humpback whales.

Later that day I went to Hatteras and there was the famed Hatteras fishing fleet tied up snug to the docks. Foreman became a wiser and wiser man as the day went on and I realized just how miserable it would have been on the high seas.

I didn't get to see a whale. But I did see something else. I got to watch the sun come up from the top of the Bonner Bridge, straight up out of a very rough and tumble Oregon Inlet.

There was one consolation, I didn't get seasick all day.

Scouting and Childhood Memories

It is one of those litanies of childhood you never forget:

"A Scout is trustworthy, loyal, helpful, friendly, courteous, kind, obedient, cheerful, thrifty, brave, clean and reverent."

I hadn't spoken those words in 25 years, but when I read about the 74th anniversary of the Boy Scouts of America, they came back in a rush. Those words were a part of my life for a decade, a decade spent in scouting.

I was not a particularly good Scout. I never made Eagle, the highest rank in scouting. I never made the Order of the Arrow, scouting's honor group.

I was just one of the minions, one of those Scouts in the back who never accomplished very much. If memory serves, the only merit badges I ever earned were camping, hiking and basket weaving.

I didn't put a lot into scouting, but I got a lot out of it.

Troop 350, sponsored by the Five Points Missionary Baptist Church, was my troop. We mostly were poor kids from Wilson's Five Points district, a blue-collar, working-class neighborhood. A lot of us didn't have uniforms, and a lot of our camping gear was owned by the troop because we couldn't afford to buy our own.

But we had something that no other troop in Wilson had. We had the Poole brothers.

Billy and Bruce Poole were our scoutmasters, and no finer men ever tried to keep kids out of trouble. They didn't always succeed, but they always tried.

Billy, now the Wilson postmaster, came as close to being an idol and a role model as I had in my youth. He is not a particularly big man. I saw him a few years ago for the first time in many years, and I was surprised how, well, ordinary looking he is. But if you'd asked me how tall he was when I was 14 years old, I would have told you his head brushed the clouds.

I lived with my elderly grandmother during those years in Five Points, and to say we were poor but proud may sound like a cliche, but it was true. I knew we were poor. Mama knew we were proud.

I don't remember the year, but it was in the mid-1950s. Summer was coming, and the troop was excited about going to camp for a week.

I was excited, too. I had never been to camp. I had camped and hiked with the troop, and I loved it, but a week of summer camp, with the canoes and swimming and bonfires and crafts and ghost stories by the campfire and all that, seemed like a dream too good to come true.

I went home excited to tell Mama that we were going to Camp Charles for a week. Camp Charles was only 15 miles up the road, but to me it seemed as far away and exotic as the jungles of Africa.

Mama asked me how much it cost. I told her it was $25 for a week. She didn't seem as excited as I was when I told her.

The truth was, we didn't have $25, and I knew that, but it didn't seem to matter. I didn't want reality to cloud my dreams. I wanted to go to camp more than anything I'd ever wanted.

I don't know how it happened, whether Billy called Mama or Mama called Billy, but when the bus loaded up in the church parking lot, I was there, going to camp.

It wasn't until many years later that I learned that Billy had paid the $25 for me to go to camp.

I don't think I ever spent a better week in my life. We hiked to a mysterious place called High Rock. I was taught to swim that summer. I had my first outing in a canoe. I slept in a three-sided building called an Adirondack cabin.

And I saw a sight that I still remember almost 30 years later.

It was the Order of the Arrow initiation ceremony. We gathered in a natural amphitheater with log benches. There was a big bonfire laid but not lighted.

We were dead silent. An Indian call echoed across the lake.

All at once, a flaming arrow came down through the sky and hit the bonfire. It burst into flames, and I almost fainted from the excitement. It may sound silly now, but it was the most impressive thing I had ever seen, and to be truthful, I can't think of a thing since then that moved me that much.

Billy, I remember the skills you taught me during those years in scouting. I can still build a campfire with no more than two matches ("The wood must be dry but from a tree," you said.) Any time I am in the woods, I bring out more trash than I take in. I can roll a sleeping bag, hang a jungle hammock and pitch a tent. I can move through the woods quietly. In fact, I taught other guys to do those things in the Army because of what you taught me.

That hamburger patty with sliced carrots, onions and potatoes all wrapped up in aluminum foil and cooked over a fire is still one of my favorite dishes.

I remember the other things you taught me, like when you help someone do it for their benefit, not your own. You don't have to tell them you did it. They know it, you know it and that's enough.

Being a Boy Scout probably is not the answer for every young boy, but it was the answer for this rebellious, hard-headed boy. I haven't always lived up to the 12 rules of behavior we had to memorize to become a Tenderfoot, but when I didn't succeed, I knew I was wrong.

Being a Boy Scout helped teach me the right way to live. Scouting did its job quite well. That I haven't always followed the rules I was taught was my responsibility. I knew right from wrong — especially when I was wrong.

Happy anniversary Boy Scouts, and thanks.

How to Face the Basement Monster

I woke up Thursday feeling like I had insulted Mr. T's mama and was paying the price.

Serves you right, I told myself, you ought to know better than to go out and party all night in the middle of the week. You deserve to feel like this, you degenerate.

Wait a minute, myself pointed out, you didn't do anything but watch a televised basketball game and go to bed early. And Carolina won. You should be feeling great.

I dragged my battered body from my heated waterbed and went to take a shower. I must be having chills, I said to myself as I stood shivering in the shower. No, fool, you're not having chills, myself said back to me, there ain't no blankety-blank hot water.

So I dried off, threw on a robe, grabbed the flashlight and went to the basement to do battle with the hot water heater. This sort of thing is a regular occurence in my charming, turn-of-the-century cottage in one of Raleigh's historic districts. We pay the price to be chic.

There is no light in the front part of my basement, but I've been down there to relight that hot water heater often enough to know that nothing is in the way if you take a sharp left at the bottom of the steps.

I took that sharp left.

And I screamed for the first time that miserable morning.

I don't know how deep the water was. I do know that it was cold, oh my goodness it was cold. And the basement floor, normally hard-packed earth, was slimy and muddly.

I stepped off the bottom step into this black morass. My stupid brain let me take a full step before it told me I was standing in ice-cold water with frozen stuff oozing between my toes.

I tried to lift both feet at once. That didn't work very well.

I tried to turn around to get back to the high ground of the steps. That didn't work very well either.

I slipped, or perhaps I simply panicked and lost all control of my flash-frozen legs and feet. And when I grabbed for the stairs, I dropped my flashlight.

The little sucker shone under water at least until I reached for it. Then it went out.

Boy was it ever dark, standing there in the frozen muck.

I made it back to the steps. Then I realized I had to get the flashlight that was lost Down There in the Dark Waters.

It became very important for me to get that flashlight. In retrospect I'm not sure why. I mean, including batteries, I know I didn't have $5 in the thing, and if you had offered me $5 to stick my little hands in that cold, slimy mess, I would have laughed at you.

But I wanted my flashlight. I had to have my flashlight.

I tried kneeling on the bottom step and reaching down as far as I could. That didn't work.

So I bravely stepped back into the dark water. No, that's a lie — I did it, but not bravely.

I didn't know at the time what I stepped on. Whatever it was, it moved.

It moved almost as fast I did. As I was going up the steps, the thought occurred to me, "I don't know what it was, but if it can live and move in muddy icy water in my basement in January, it is tougher than I am."

I was standing in my kitchen, shivering and taking stock of the damage. Forget the feet, they are so cold they will obviously have to be amputated.

I was wet and muddy from just below the knees to the floor. The floor itself was just as wet and muddy as my legs.

And the bottom 2 inches of my velour robe was no great shakes either. (If I hear one snicker about my velour robe, somebody is in trouble.)

My head hurt, my feet were numb, my flashlight was lost Down There in the Dark Waters, and something was alive in my basement. I wanted my mama to come tuck me into bed and make me some chicken soup and buy me a coloring book.

Then I got mad. Boy, did I get mad. I went storming into the bedroom, leaving muddy prints in my wake, and put on my clothes and my combat boots. I was going to kill the monster that lived Down There in the Dark Waters.

I stomped down the stairs to the dark basement making all the noise I could. I wanted the monster to know I was coming for him.

I splashed into the water without a thought for my own personal safety. Take that, basement monster.

I felt him beneath my combat boot. I had him. Eat cold leather, sucker.

I ended up having to throw the flashlight away.

The first time, I stepped on it with my bare feet I had just rolled it through the muck.

But that last time, when I stepped on it with my combat boot, well, that did it, I bent the case, and it won't work anymore.

I was so mad that I went out and jumped into the car and tore off to the store like a muddy fiend and bought another flashlight, rushed home, waded through the flooded basement — ignoring my personal safety — and made it to the hot water heater. The pilot light had just that moment appeared above water as the flood slowly receded.

I lit the hot water heater, went back upstairs and made myself a cup of coffee. While it was perking, I went through the mail.

The first thing I found was my gas bill — you know, the stuff that lets me have heat and hot water every morning?

I opened it slowly as the memory of all those bitter cold days and nights came back to me. Boy, I'll bet this is going to be high, I thought.

I screamed for the second time that miserable morning.

This is Rogers' Law of Survival: Any morning when you wake up feeling sick and have to wade through freezing water and oozing mud in your bare feet and lose your flashlight and ruin the kitchen floor and make a mess out of your favorite robe and have no hot water for a shower and get a gas bill of $193 and scream twice, that day is going to be a rotten day. You ought to go back to bed and pull the covers up over your head and forget it for 24 hours.

So I did.

Stunned by a Shot at Stardom

Manteo

I still don't know what happened to the limousine.

I mean, it isn't all that important, and I'm trying to be gracious about it. But, after all, aren't limousines expected for us bigtime move stars?

When Jim Coleman from the Department of Cultural Resources asked me to star in his movie, I naturally assumed that I would get the full star treatment.

I did not expect to wind up looking like a blue Smurfs reject.

I am the star of this epic, by the way. I'm not exactly sure how they're going to do it, since I only had one line and maybe five seconds on camera. It might take some creative editing to redo the whole thing to feature me, but I have full confidence in Jim.

There were some rumors that I wasn't the star, that the movie we were making is about a bunch of guys who sailed to the New World from England 400 years ago and I was nothing but an extra. But I discounted the rumors, as jealous backbiting by my supporting cast. You know how petty actors are.

Why else would I have put up with unspeakable discomfort — this thing was shot on Saturday afternoon during the Carolina-Temple basketballgame, to say nothing of the second-degree frostbite to portions of my body that no sane man would want frostbitten — unless I was the star?

I certainly hope they don't think I did it for that one stupid line they gave me to say: "This fresh wind may yet carry us to the New World."

We were filming aboard the beautiful Elizabeth II, the replica of the ship that brought Sir Walter Raleigh's band of colonists to Roanoke Island several years ago.

Jim is the director of a series of 120 one-minute films to be shown on statewide television throughout this year as part of the state's 400th anniversary celebration.

The project is a combined effort of the North Carolina Association of Broadcasters, the UNC Center for Public Television, the Department of Cultural Resources and the Pepsi-Cola bottlers of North Carolina.

Jim invited me to take part in the last day's filming. Figuring that this would be my big chance to be discovered by some Hollywood mogul, I agreed.

We began, as do all actors, in makeup. I naturally assumed that because I was going to be the star, I would wind up looking sort of like Errol Flynn in "Captain Blood." But makeup artist Alex Constantion of Richmond, Va., had other ideas.

"We want you to look like the early stages of scurvy," he said. Scurvy? How am I going to woo a lusty wench with nasty looking bumps on my face and a livid red scar down my right cheek?

Then it was on to costumes. I expected silk, lace and satin. I got rags.

Doug Varger, the costumer from Winston-Salem, figured that my natural leading-man sex appeal didn't need textile help, I suppose.

Once aboard the Elizabeth II, I met my supporting cast. These guys were real sailors, part of the volunteer crew that will sail the Elizabeth II once they figure out how to get it out of Manteo's Shallowbag Bay. Coleman decided to use them because they know the difference between a rope and a line and can say things like "belay the mizzen."

These guys — Bill Dunn of Washington, John Vang of Raleigh, Jimmy Barger of Manteo and Hiram Gallop of Greenville — are some of the best actors I've seen.

The idea was that we are in the doldrums in July (becalmed is what the sailors called it), that it is hot, and we are not moving.

Suddenly, a wind comes up and I utter my line, "This fresh wind may yet carry us to the New World."

OK, so it ain't, "Here's looking at you, kid," but you should have heard my reading. I was coached in the proper dialect by Bob Mills, another professional supporting actor who is playing the small part of Sir Walter Raleigh. The man thinks he's the star or something. I tried not to disappoint him.

Well, it wasn't July, and we were not becalmed. It was March and 40 degrees, and the wind was huffing and puffing out of the frigid northeast at 35 mph, and we were barefooted and dressed in loose-fitting clothes. Stand in a freezing gale sometime and try to "act hot," as one smart aleck in coat, gloves and scarf said.

We did that sucker in one take — that's show biz lingo for getting it right the first time — but Coleman, the sadistic director, made us do it again. I didn't complain, mind you, because the second take was to film my close-up. I figured that's what was going to get me a big Hollywood contract, a date with Loni Anderson and a wig like Burt Reynolds'.

The series is on all commercial and public television stations in the state.

Watch for me. I'm the ragged-looking, scurvy-encrusted, scarred bilge pumper who gives the big line.

Of course, I plan to be in Hollywood by then, so I'll probably miss it.

Looking for That Sweet Revenge

The more I think about it, the angrier I get.

I am a victim of a crime for the first time, and it is a lot more disturbing than I thought it would be.

It was a petty crime, and my financial loss was minimal. I was not insured, and my property was not seriously damaged.

I suppose I should be thankful it wasn't worse.

But I'm not. I'm angry.

I didn't notice it at first. I walked out to my car as I do every morning. I felt particularly good because the sun was shining and the radio weather announcer had told me the day would be in the mid-80s, the first incredibly gorgeous day in a spring beset with rotten weather.

I had a trip planned to enjoy the day, a trip that ended up not being as much fun as I'd hoped.

Wonder how that happened, I thought, looking at the open glove compartment. I didn't remember opening it, and I know I didn't dump all the junk on the floor like that. Maybe the catch broke and the weight of the maps, car papers, extra pencils and notebooks made it fall open. Sure, and frogs fly.

It is amazing how long it takes to realize you've been hit by a crime. It is the last possibility you consider, even when faced by the obvious evidence. I was sitting there thinking of rational and irrational answers, and none of them included someone breaking into my car.

Finally, it hit me. My car had been broken into.

I was miffed at first and a little stunned but not worried because there was nothing in the glove compartment of any value.

Once I realized what must have happened, I quickly checked to make sure my stereo still was in place. It was.

Then I felt for my briefcase behind the seat. It was there.

How odd, I thought, to break into a car and not take anything. Oh well, forget it. But I couldn't forget it.

It took me a full 30 minutes to realize that my citizens band radio was gone. In fact, I didn't notice it until I looked to see what was hitting my foot while I was driving and realized it was a black cable I had not seen before. It was the CB antenna cable and it wasn't hooked to anything.

The anger came slowly. At first, I tried to rationalize it. I'd had that radio for almost seven years, and in the past few years, I probably didn't even turn it on more than twice a year. I'd never miss it. It wasn't even worth calling the police. No big deal.

But the more I drove, the more the feeling in my gut changed from being shocked to being miffed to being outright angry.

Then, the feelings I had heard other crime victims describe suddenly made sense. I really did feel violated.

How dare that lowlife piece of trash break into my car!

That was my car, not his. That was my radio, not his.

What gave him the right to take something that belonged to me? Who does he think he is?

As I drove, I kept thinking, "That rotten scum probably sat in the seat where I'm sitting to reach down and rip my radio from under the dash."

Someone, while I slept not 20 yards away, had decided to take something that belonged to me. He made a conscious decision to do it. It wasn't merely lying on the sidewalk so he could pick it up.

Oh, how I so wish I had known he was here.

I called the police, knowning full well that the radio was gone for all time.

But that wasn't why I called. I don't even want the thing back — somehow that inanimate object has been sullied, and I'm not sure I'd ever want it back in my car — but I want that sucker caught.

I want him to know exactly what I think of him. I want more than anything to sit in a courtroom and watch that lowlife sweat bullets. I know, he won't go to jail. Even if they caught him with the radio in his hand, he'd probably get off with a suspended sentence. But I want him to sit in a courtroom and worry that maybe this time he won't get off, maybe this will be the time he'll hear the jail door slam.

I don't care whether it was just a kid on a lark. I don't care how poor he is. I don't care what he is. I have no pity for him.

I want revenge.

He has made me feel not quite as comfortably secure as once I felt. I sat on my front porch that night, enjoying the spring evening, but I found myself staring at my car a lot. I found myself glancing at the car every time I passed a window.

Every time I heard a noise, I got up to make sure my car was all right.

I don't like feeling that paranoia. And he did that to me when he opened my car door and sat down in my seat and put his hands on my radio.

He violated my sense of security, and I owe him one for that. That secure feeling was infinitely more valuable than a 7-year-old CB radio that might net him $10 at some local fence. Oh, how I hope that fence is an undercover police front.

I probably won't get the chance to settle the score, but the thought that I might — that by calling the police they might keep a close eye on the neighborhood and since he got away with it once maybe he'll get cocky and try it again and they'll catch him — gives me a ray of hope.

I'm just a little harder than I was before, and I don't like feeling like that.

Revenge is not sweet, but I sure do want a taste of that bitter brew.

After a Life-or-Death Choice

His name was Willie. He was a too-fat cat that began life as a cute bundle of white fur. He grew into a clown and eventually into a rambunctious terror who left scars on all who came to visit.

Then he got sick.

The decision to have a pet put to death is a difficult one.

You can use all the comforting words you want. You can say your pet is being "put to sleep." You can say you're putting your pet "out of his misery," that he will be better off for what you do.

But the simple fact remains that you are playing God, deciding that another life, completely under your control, should end. And at night, when you lie there in the darkness, all the good intentions don't seem to mean much. That's when the doubts begin.

Could he have been saved? Did I have to do it now? Was I being selfish? Did I do it for him or for me?

Willie's illness came just as he was maturing into a handsome devil who posed and preened and accepted praise for his good looks as if it were his due. He was gorgeous, and he knew it.

He was 10 months old and glowing with good heatlh, or so we thought.

Cat owners sometimes feel a little foolish taking a cat to a veterinarian with no symptoms other than "he just isn't himself."

But Willie wasn't himself. His appetite seemed to fade. Always a big eater, he began merely to nibble.

He always met everyone at the front door, coming on a run from wherever he might have been destroying something at the moment.

But he began lying in one spot on the sofa, barely raising his head when someone came to the door.

He didn't chase his buddy Waylon any more. The ball with the bell that would occupy him for hours lay still in the corner.

Willie walked slowly, it seemed, and he felt awfully hot.

I really wan't prepared for what veterinarian Les Tremaine said. I expected a virus, perhaps, or some other mystical disease that could be cured in a week and make Willie once again the cat I could get so mad at when he and Waylon played tag at 2 a.m. and the bed where I was trying to sleep was home base.

I was not expecting cancer.

It is called feline leukemia, and it kills cats. It also is highly contagious among cats.

Les said that Willie might hang on awhile longer but that he'd never be what he had been. And he could infect any cat that came in contact with him.

I didn't want Willie to suffer. He had been too good a cat to go through that. He had given too much love and too many laughs ever to be in pain.

And I didn't want his disease to spread among other cats in the neighborhood. He stayed indoors, but, there always was a chance that he might slip out. I was hurting, and I didn't want other pet owners to go through what I was going through.

And I was selfish. I didn't want to watch him slowly die in front of my eyes, wasting away as the cancer took its toll.

I didn't want to look every day in Willie's eyes and not know whether he was in pain.

I made the decision, finally. I told Les to kill Willie.

But I still wonder some times. Who was I trying to keep from suffering? Whose welfare was uppermost in my mind?

I'll miss Willie a long time. I know it is silly, but sometimes I feel like he's still here. Something seems to move out of the corner of my eye. Sometimes I awake when something jumps on the foot of the bed and for a second I know it's Willie, but he's never there when I look. Probably just a dream.

But you know, I like those moments. I like to think Willie, or my conscience, is letting me know I did the right thing.

Cloudy Night at the Gator Bowl

I drove 1,000 miles to see the University of North Carolina play the University of Arkansas in the Gator Bowl in Jacksonville, Fla., Dec. 28.

It cost me a ton of money.

You sat home and watched the game on television. What did you spend altogether, maybe five bucks for chips, dip and beer?

So tell me, how'd we look? I haven't the foggiest idea.

That's not right. I do have a foggy idea. What I don't have is a clear idea.

I'm sorry, I know that's an awful pun but I couldn't resist.

But if you had had a vacation like the one I just finished (and there you were making all those unkind Johnny Carson jokes about me being on vacation all the time) you'd be desperate for laughs, too.

Yes, friends, I was one of the lucky 25,000 North Carolinians who got to go to Florida over the holidays and see our beloved Tar Heels play football.

I thought it sounded like a good idea. Breeze down to the old Sunshine State, catch a game and breeze back.

I seemed to be the only person who noticed that it was pouring down rain when we hit the road. Traffic on Interstate 95 certainly didn't notice. It roared along at 75 miles an hour in the fast lane, a relatively slow 70 in the slow lane.

I am not exaggerating. I'm making 75 just to keep from being run over. It was pouring down rain, everyone had their windshield wipers running full out and we were screaming down the highway, bumper to bumper, like a pack of suicidal maniacs.

It was a sight to behold. Totally panicked little old men were hunched over their steering wheels like obsessed teenagers on a video game. It had an unreal quality to it. No one dared look left or right. It was one blink and you're dead. White knuckles all the way.

I heard truck drivers on my CB swear it was the heaviest traffic in memory. A combination of Carolina fans, Floridians heading home from the holidays, vacationers heading to Florida to escape the season's first snow up north, a Sunday afternoon and rainy weather had joined forces to kill us all.

We blew by a cop in Georgia that actually got on the CB channel and urged us to keep it moving, keep it moving, don't slow down to look at the wreck just up the road. I'm doing 75 and this yahoo is telling me to speed up?

At least I didn't get sleepy.

The plan in Florida was simple. Stay with friends, kill Monday and head out early for the game. We made a dry run during the day so we'd be able to find the stadium. We even had a Jacksonville native and resident riding shotgun. I was to drive.

We left at 6:30 p.m., figuring to arrive at the stadium by 7, have us a little tailgate party (my car doesn't have a tailgate, but we faked it) and then hit the stands at 8 for a 9 kickoff.

There was nowhere to park two hours before game time. We lapped the stadium three times, following the rather pushy directions of traffic cops. On the third lap I yelled and asked where we were to park. Keep moving, I was told. I was not encouraged.

Finally I made a mistake, took a wrong turn and was directed into a large field (for punishment, I suppose). We were herded into a large mass of automobiles jammed 12 inches apart. No lanes or anything like that. Just a field full of cars in every direction. When the field was full they locked the gate behind us and never came back.

Our plan had a flaw. By the time we headed for the game, two of our band were, to put it delicately, drunk as skunks. They were the only ones who knew how to get home.

You've probably heard enough about the fog from other sources. It was real thick. From my seats high in the end zone — I lied to myself and told myself they would be good seats since I could see patterns develop and stuff like that and myself did not believe me for very long — I saw little that went on at midfield and nothing that happened beyond the 50-yard line. Guess where everything happened?

Mostly I listened to the game to know what was happening. If they yelled Razorback cheers I looked sad. If I heard Tar Heel cheers I looked happy.
The two drunks looked drunk.

I heard my school's song after the game so we won and headed for the field of cars. After an hour I still was sitting there, wondering when the traffic would begin to move and wondering where I was going when it did.

My friends were snoring softly in the arms of demon rum, I was stuck in traffic with 70,000 people in a city I knew nothing about, the fog was ghastly, I was hopelessly lost and I had to go to the bathroom.

I woke up our guide a few times. All he would, or could, say was "go straight." No matter where we were, no matter in what direction we were headed. No matter that straight ahead was the St. John's River. Go straight.

God must be, as the bumper stickers say, a Tar Heel because we made it somehow, only to arise the next morning for the trip home after four hours sleep.
It still was raining. Still is, probably.

Life of the Short-Distance Runner

I don't like to lie on official government documents, but I told a lie the other day, a bald-faced lie.

I didn't know it was a lie then. I thought that at most I was slightly embellishing the facts, but it turned out to be a real first-class fib.

What I did was sign a statement that I was in good physical condition.

You had to sign it to participate in the fifth annual Governor's Run for Fun and Health.

I had been in serious training for this little 1.25-mile gallop through Historic Oakwood and I just knew I was ready.

I ran in the first of these events five years ago. I did not do too well. I was passed by children. I was passed by a man wearing a gray gabardine suit and black wingtips. I was passed by a man in a wheelchair.

I swore that would never happen again.

So I went into training.

I figured that since I was exhausted at the end of the first run, the thing to do was rest up for the second one.

So I rested.

For five years, I have rested. I have not run at all, saving my strength for my triumphant return to competiton. The only running I did at all during those five long years of serious training was while playing softball, and since I didn't get too many hits, I didn't have to run a lot.

I made sure I didn't waste my strength. I would not run from the car to the house in the rain. I sat there and waited for it to clear. I strolled sedately those few times when I wasn't sitting.

I figured I had saved up a lot of strength in five years, surely enough to get me through Oakwood with respectable dash, flash and class.

I was serious about this thing. I had made tactical errors my first time, errors I swore not to repeat.

For example, this time I had promised myself I would not stop and have a cigarette at the halfway point. My plan this time was to smoke several before the contest began and then tough it out.

This time, remembering the fellow in the gray suit and black shoes, I decided not to dress in runner's garb. I showed up in jeans, a dress shirt, a sweater, black socks and sneakers.

But I had a secret weapon. I had my Willie Nelson headband. I had noticed that other people who seemed to do well wore headbands. Some of them had headbands with the word "Head" emblazoned on them. I figured it was unnecessary to label my head, since I thought most people would recognize it as a head, what with the ears and a nose. They are difficult to mistake.

Besides, I did not want to be taken to the hospital in shorts and a smelly T-shirt. I like to be properly dressed at all times.

I was a finely honed machine when I got to the starting line. People around me were stretching and jogging in place. I had stretched that morning when I got out of bed and more seemed redundant.

I followed my game plan. I sat down and smoked a cigarette. Then, just to make sure, I smoked another one.

Gov. James B. Hunt Jr. made a few remarks that no one heard because he was at the back of the pack with a Mister Microphone. He made the runners wait until he got to the front of the pack, a cheap move that bears investigating. I thought that was cheating and plan to file a complaint.

We athletes watch for things like that.

Then came the echo of a gunshot and everybody hauled off down the hill.

Lord have mercy, I was almost trampled by 2,000 thundering feet. Naked legs flashed by me in a blur.

I put out my final cigarette and took off, so confident I may have even appeared cocky to the cheering bystanders.

I ran with ease for a long time. Wow, I had it made, this would be my final revenge.

I began to tire after awhile and looked up to see how close I was to the finish line.

I wasn't all that close to the finish line.

In fact, I hadn't quite reached the starting line.

But on I struggled, a gallant athlete giving it his all, running not for fame and riches but for the glory of sport. I'm sure that the bystanders went away inspired by my effort.

It was Rocky IV.

Then my valiant heart gave out.

Courtney Overby is her name and she has blond hair and it was all her fault.

She blew by me like Wonder Woman, her strong legs flying in the humid afternoon.

The smart aleck 3½-year-old child was on a Hot Wheels tricycle.

I looked behind me to see whether I had a chance to beat anybody — I didn't care who it was — but the only person behind me was Deborah Pope and she was five months pregnant and she was gaining on me with every step.

So I did what any red-blooded American would do when faced with such a crisis.

I cheated.

I took a short cut.

Gosh, I was clever.

I cut over one street just in time to see the leaders in the race flash past. I walked a block and when I thought no one was looking I stepped off the cub and, with head held high, dashed for the finish line. I tried to look appropriately tired and sweaty.

That's when I saw Courtney Overby gain.

She was going uphill this time but it didn't seem to matter. There she went, two feet high and flying past me

I was not last. I did beat Deborah Pope and her unborn baby by several yards.

And I didn't have to trip her to do it.

But I was fully prepared to, if necessary.

Impressing (Compressing) the Press

Pope Air Force Base

The U.S. Air Force did its blue-suited best to impress the visiting reporters.

It tried so hard to impress us, in fact, that it danged near killed us all in a variety of interesting ways.

Most spectacular of those was the old falling jeep trailer trick, although six of us came pretty close to getting hit in the helicopter emergency landing that took place moments after we got off the ill-fated bird.

I won't even go into the heat stroke and the crazed helicopter pilots who tried to give us all heart attacks by flying with the doors open and their whirlybirds tilted over on their sides so we would get a great view of the ground.

The idea was to bring together reporters from all over the country to watch the Air Force choose the best Military Airlift Command crews in the world in a week of competition.

Reporters were flown in from all over the United States to witness all of this. They flew on Air Force planes from places like Missouri, Texas, Arkansas, and South Carolina.

We were all suitably impressed until the jeep trailer almost fell on our heads from 75 feet in the air.

We were out in the dusty wasteland of Fort Bragg's drop zones. We were there to watch crews of C-130 transport planes drop 700-pound jeep trailers by parachute while flying at a speed of 130 knots. The winner would be the crew that dropped the load closest to the target, in this case a big letter "C" outlined with red panels on the ground.

I noticed that a lot of military people were standing around the big C as we walked up, along with a couple of jeeps.

"Where do you want us to stand?" I asked Air Force Capt. B.L. "Buzz" Howard, my escort. Air Force pilots like nicknames like "Buzz."

"Stand right here," said Buzz, pointing to the gathering around the target.

"But isn't that the target?" I asked, trying not to act too wimpy in the presence of so much macho.

"Yes, and it's the safest place," he said. "They never hit the target."

You want to know what it is even dumber than telling us to stand right on the target?

We believed him and stood right there on that target like a pack of idiots while they tried to hit us with falling trailers.

They never hit the target, huh?

Tell that to the crew of the C-130 from the 907th Tactical Airlift Group from Columbus, Ohio.

We watched several crews drop their loads, and it was really impressive. They came in low, and a drogue parachute came out the back of the plane, followed by a jeep trailer on a platform which soon dangled beneath a large cargo parachute.

They floated to earth hither and yon, and Buzz was right, they never hit the target.

Then came those flying fools from the 907th.

I will always remember Buzz's fateful words.

"Boy, they've sure got a nice approach," he said as the C-130 came straight at us over the tree line.

Out came the drogue chute, out came the trailer on the platform and pop went the cargo chute and down it came.

Straight at the target.

We waited for the trailer to drift to one side or the other of the target where we were standing.

It got closer and closer, heading straight for the assembled press, two jeeps and a goodly number of military men.

"Follow me," shouted Buzz and all the other press escorts, who then proceeded to run back and forth in all directions. One thought we ought to go this way, then he'd look up and decide that wasn't right, we ought to go that way.

People were bumping into each other, falling down, all the time looking up at the jeep trailer that by this time seemed to be blocking out most of the sky as it came right at us.

"To heck with this," I said and took off.

We didn't look very cool, scrambling around in the face of impending doom but Air Force Maj. Gen. Donald Bennett and Lt. Gen. Bob Coverdale were super cool. They stood there, rock steady, looking up at the descending trailer above their heads.

They finally came to their senses and decided they were going to die if they kept standing there being cool and brave, so right at the last second they ran like the rest of us chickens.

Unfortunately, Bennett chose that moment to fall down and came within about 12 inches of being the first Air Force general in history to be jeep-trailered to death.

Coverdale, who looks for all the world like Steve Canyon of comic strip fame and is, in fact, called Steve Canyon behind his back by young officers, messed up his spiffy tailored blue coveralls, and got dirt all over his highly spit-shined or perhaps patent leather shoes. His white scarf was in total disarray but his sunglasses never moved.

What a guy.

It was quiet just for a moment as we all thanked our lucky stars we were not dead.

Someone said he could hear the sound of laughter from the crew of the C-130, the guys they said would never hit the target, but I didn't hear them.

I was feeling sort of bad for the immaculate Coverdale and his now-dusty dignity until lunch when he stood up in front of us all and said a dumb thing.

He called these current days of no war, the time normal people thankfully call peace, "the precontingency phase" so I figured he deserved to scramble in the dirt.

Family and Friends

Dawn is a good time to drive from Raleigh to Louisburg, especially if it is a golden dawn that promises sunshine after a week of rain.

The land rolls to a misty horizon where a fat, red sun is hitting its stride and drying a soggy winter earth.

Obviously, this is to be a day of only good things. That's what I was thinking, anyway. Actually, what I was trying to do was justify getting up at 5 a.m. to eat fish.

The streets of Louisburg were quiet when I pulled up to the courthouse. I was looking for directions to the fire station and that seemed a good place to start. I rolled down the window and knew I was near.

There are only two odors that will penetrate eight inches of cement block — chitlins and salt herring in hot grease. They also are the only two odors that you can identify the first time you smell them.

I knew I had found breakfast.

There they were, sizzling in the grease right beside the bright red fire truck, dozens of salt herring.

How, I asked Mayor V.A. Peoples, did he convince John Gilliam, Elias Murphy Jr. and Cardain Murphy to get up before dawn and stand over a tub of those stinking fish?

"They're herring lovers," Hizoner said. "You promise them a herring, and they'll do anything. These fellows are Franklin Countians, and to be a Franklin Countian you have to love chitlins and herring."

Seems a high price to pay. Franklin County is without a doubt a great place to live, but chitlins and salt herring?

Fortunately for me and the rest of the folks with reasonable stomachs, chitlins weren't on the menu for this particular feast. But herring . . .

The herring is a bony fish that swims up North Carolina rivers, particularly the Roanoke, to make babies as spring approaches. Just as sure as fish swim, men catch them. You can fill a bushel basket in 10 minutes on a slow day with nothing more than a dip net — which leaves the lucky fisherman with a problem.

Fish rot, you see, with some speed, so fishermen came up with the idea that if you packed the little fellows in salt brine, they would be preserved. It apparently never occurred to anyone that there was no particular reason to preserve them in the first place since they are terribly bony, but preserve them they did.

And once they had them preserved, some brave soul ate one and discovered two things: The salt makes the bones so soft you can eat right through them, and they don't taste all that good.

The early morning eating of salt herring is tradition in Louisburg, going back further than any one I ran into could remember.

The mayor began giving these herring breakfasts some years back — everybody had a different idea of how many years ago it all began — and the semiannual gathering of a few close friends has grown into a large crowd of close friends jammed into the second floor of the fire station.

So it came to pass that this year, we all gathered, a few lies were swapped, a tale or two told and right on the button at 7:30 a.m., the chief cook and firefighter came through the door with white enamel dishpans piled high with golden herring.

The blessing was asked and the mayor, since he pays the bills, got to get up and say a few words. He said, "We've got two undertakers and one doctor here, so enjoy yourself."

They did. These good old country boys and girls, each of whom swore they were raised on salt herring for breakfast, tore into them.

Some people ate several. I don't know how or why.

I ate one. Boy, was I full in a hurry.

They aren't all that bad; they're just all that salty.

How salty are they?

Tell you what you do: Take a box of salt and pour it on the table. Now take a spoon and eat it.

Salt herrings are saltier than that.

But the company was terrific. And that's the whole idea.

Silvery Send-Off for Summer

Laurel Mill

It was the last day of summer 1982.

History will recall that it was an unexpectedly chilly, damp day. Some would call it dreary, but they would be wrong.

The sky was soft silver, almost the color of the tattered old sweater I pulled out of the bottom drawer, where it had lain for months. It felt nice, like an old friend's hug.

It was a day for slow drives down back roads, for savoring subtle beauty while the car stereo played blues guitar.

There was no sadness in the drizzle and fog. The earth was cuddled in a gentle blanket of silver down. It was the last day of summer, and the time of rest had come.

The colors of autumn were spread like an artist's palette — softened, less garish, more tasteful in the gentle gloom.

There was the tan of languishing fields, their work done for another year. There was the dramatic black of Angus cattle silhouetted against yellow-green pastures in the gray fog. And there were the smiles of tiny yellow wildflowers dancing on the roadside.

There were orange pumpkins, those harbingers of hobgoblins and home cooking, dotting the field along U.S. 401. Even the mighty green kudzu signaled its annual surrender with little flags of yellow leaves.

Tobacco stalks stood stripped, the few remaining leaves a deep gold, the stalks black-brown. Long-dried corn stalks, dusty amber, drooped in the dampness.

But it was not a time of death and decay. The John A. Perrys proudly announced the birth of a daughter with a bright pink ribbon tied to their mailbox by the side of the shiny, wet highway.

Summer with all its sensuous beauty, is like a cocktail party with too many people trying too hard to be clever amid the music turned up too loud. But its last day this year was made for quiet reverie among old friends.

This day's friends would be Bill Holmes and the old mill he runs — and we both love — in Sandy Creek.

We pulled up chairs in the mill, built in the early 1800s, and listened to the rush of water over the dam, the smell of golden corn around us. Like millers of another time, Bill will grind the corn into wonderful meal for his friends and neighbors.

We talked of his 32 years in Detroit before coming home to buy and clean up the old mill where he had played as a child. Dogs slept at our feet.

We spoke of baptizings in the creek, the two weddings held in this most beautiful of places and the mud wrestling party the students from Louisburg College held this summer. We watched a skilled angler pull a flashing silver fish from the tumbling, foaming water.

I made fun of his outhouse, the finest in Franklin County, an improvement that raised the tax value of the mill by $10,000.

Mostly, we sat and enjoyed the misty day and each other's company and allowed as how water running over a dam is better than any sleeping pill.

Bill told me that since December he has put 312 miles on his car.

"Why go anywhere else when you're in the best place there is?" he asked. Bill and Margaret are happy in their old mill, and I'm happy for them. They are nice people who share their gentle paradise with all who come to call.

I felt a need to walk in his woods, and Bill understood that. So I left him with his dogs and eased my way into the quiet, wet forest.

Over here, peeking up through the dark forest floor, was a toadstool of coral and cream; over there, one of alabaster.

Before me was a strand of exquisite crystal, a spider web hung with pearls of mist. I watched a spider lumber to safety with his catch before I walked on.

There were clusters of toadstools that looked like mounds of caramel candy, and I thought of the State Fair.

There were bright red berries, and I thought of Christmas.

There was quiet and peace and solitude. Over a hilltop, down the road from a cemetery, gray smoke drifted from a stone chimney over a farmhouse that never has felt a paint brush on its gray-brown sides.

I thanked Bill for saving Laurel Mill and sharing it with me.

The sun came out as I drove home in late afternoon, shoving its way through the clouds.

Some people would have said the last day of summer was better then.

I liked it better in the mist.

Winning Stew of Food, Friends

Ayden

Pat Tripp posed an interesting question:

"Do you think we're putting too much emphasis on eating in Ayden? We've got the Collard Festival, we're famous for our barbecue and now everybody will know about our famous fish stew."

Ah yes, the legendary Ayden fish stew, a hearty repast served in the luxurious shop of Tripp's Tire Service in the finest paper bowls money can buy by highly trained gourmet, chefs (the combined age of the two cooks and one helper is 221 years). Take the stuff to Paris and call it bouillabaisse. This stew, as my daddy used to say, will put hair on your chest.

The estimates vary, but it is safe to say that a thousand or so kettles of fish stew have been cooked at Bert Tripp's tire palace in the past 25 years, most of them under the close supervision of Wilbur Walls, 78, the senior cook.

"Why do we do it?" Wilbur asked rhetorically when I asked him the same question. "We just love fish stew, that's why."

That's good enough for me. No heavy answers, just the truth. These old boys love their fish stew.

Wilbur and his co-cook Claude Burney, 76, are daily fixtures at Tripps, the closest thing to a general store you'll find in town.

"If they're not here by 8:30 or so I call them to make sure they're all right," owner Bert Tripp said. "They come down here every day to sit and argue and pick at each other."

And on Tuesdays, especially in the winter, they cook up a pot of fish stew, using the same recipe that has been used in these parts for years.

It all started 25 years ago when Larry Tripp, Bert's daddy, ran the place. He and Wilbur and Wilbur's brother Jim, who died last year, used to get together and cook 'em a mess of fish stew in the shop every week and the tradition has lingered all these years.

"It used to cost $2 for a stew," said Bert, who picks up most of the tab. "Now it costs $15, but it's worth it."

Claude Burney joined the crew a few years back and has become a regular. Tyree Buck, 67, is a relative newcomer of five years and is slowly taking the place of Jim around the fire. All Claude and Wilbur let Tyree do so far is carry the heavy cast iron pot to the table.

Wilbur and Claude get the stew on about 9:30 a.m. They use an old pot that Larry found somewhere 25 years ago and worked on for a week to get rid of the rust. Into that goes a half pound of bacon that is browned. The grease is drained off. To that they add three pounds of potatoes, three pounds of onions, a small can of tomato paste and a lot of black pepper and salt. Then they add some more salt and black pepper. And then some more whenever the mood hits them.

If Bert isn't looking, Wilbur throws in some hot pepper pods.

"Now, Wilbur, you know Bert doesn't like hot pepper," Claude tells Wilbur every week.

"I know, but he eats it, don't he," Wilbur tells Claude every week.

And every week Bert takes the pepper out and puts it in Wilbur's bowl.

You cook that about an hour or so, then you add four pounds of fish, preferably rock. About 10 minutes before an hour and a half have passed, you add 15 eggs, making sure you don't break the yolks.

When it has been on for an hour and half or so you cut it off and let it sit for an hour. That lets the flavors mingle, I was told. If you use a heavy cast iron pot, it will be just at eating temperature when you get back from going to buy the corn bread.

The ritual at Tripp's is set in stone. Wilbur and Claude have rocking chairs with their names on them, and no one else takes their seats. They sit by the bubbling pot and discuss farming, friends who have died, their gardens and how much the other one does not know about fish stews and how lazy and no-account they both are.

"This is the best thing that has ever been for Claude," said his wife Verna. "I don't know what I'd do if he didn't have this place to come to. It means a lot to both of them.

"He'll come down here and cook all morning, and he can't boil water at home."

Along about 11:30 a.m., Wilbur and Claude argue about who is going to get the cornbread from either Bum Dennis' or Pete Jones' barbecue places. This day, they both went.

At 11:45, they return and find that the crowd has begun to gather. Anyone who stops by is welcome to join in the eating.

Claude cuts up the corn bread with his pocket knife, Tyree takes the pot to the table and then it is everyone for themselves.

This day, the crew included the Rev. Vic Wilson, an Englishman who is pastor of Ayden Christian Church; Wilbur's nephew, Sam Bert; Bert's wife, Pat; Mrs. Burney; and a hungry columnist who ate three bowls full and embarrassed himself with gluttony. I can't tell you how good it was because words fail me.

By tradition, the women eat in the office while the men eat in the shop.

The eating done, everyone rears back in a chair and socializes for a while until Wilbur and Claude begin to argue about who's going to clean up the mess and who gets to take home the leftovers.

Eating good food with good friends — that's the real recipe for fish stew at Tripp's.

A Friend Leaves - The Ties Stay

A good friend is hard enough to find, and a best friend is a treasure.

You can have a lot of acquaintances and a few good friends, but a best friend doesn't come along that often.

After all, you can only have one at a time, so they are valuable beyond all measure.

You can't go out and look for a best friend because you'd never recognize one when you saw it. You can spot a pretty diamond or a good bird dog, but you never know what a best friend is going to look like.

But when you find one, you'll know it.

You'll know by the way that person makes you feel when you're together. Most of all, you are completely relaxed. A best friend doesn't care whether you win, lose, or make a fool of yourself or succeed beyond your wildest dreams.

There is no pressure when you're with your best friend. Most of us have a wide streak of insecurity. We all want to be liked, and we try to do and say the right thing to make people like us.

You don't have to try when you're with your best friend. It comes naturally. You don't have to try at all. You say and do what is really you, and that's what your best friend likes.

I've been lucky because I have a best friend. We've known each other for nine years. For six of those years we have worked together.

Neither of us planned to become best friends; it just happened. We knew all the same people and went to all the same parties and found out we both liked the same things. We seemed to have a good time together.

I liked his taste in music. We both lived and died by the fortunes of the Tar Heel football and basketball teams. We shared occupations and Southern traditions.

But don't get the idea that we agree on everything. The man knows not the first thing about good barbecue, preferring the Western North Carolina variety and (gag) he puts mayo on a hamburger.

And he hates the Yankees.

But he does like to sit around and talk until 3 in the morning as the beer supply gets lower and our insights scale to new intellectual heights.

And he likes kittens.

We both learned to play golf at the same time, and he wins more that I do. I can take him at pool until he gets hot, but I blow him away on Galaxian. He thinks he's good at backgammon, but that's one I'll never concede.

We are both highly competitive, but a funny thing happens when we play against each other: It doesn't really matter who wins. Oh, we bluster a lot, but losing to my best friend doesn't hurt a bit. We applaud each other's successes and gently tease the failures. We both win because we've been together awhile.

We both have been fairly successful at what we do, and that's good because both of us take our jobs seriously. We both have the idea that our jobs are important and we both work hard at getting them right. We wouldn't have the same respect for each other if we didn't.

Both of us have been through stormy times in our lives, and when those times came, the other always was standing by. We are not big on giving each other advice because neither of us is very big on taking advice. Mostly what we do is listen to the other person talk it out and find his own solution.

My best friend has left Raleigh to move to another job in another state, but I don't fear for our friendship.

I won't be surprised when a letter from him arrives in the mail, delighted but not surprised. And he won't be surprised when I call him up just to talk. Best friends rarely surprise each other like that.

Best friendships can survive long distance. The next time we meet there won't be the searching awkwardness that comes when we re-meet old acquaintances. I'll walk into his new place, and I'll know on which side of the refrigerator shelf he keeps the beer.

When he comes to see me, he won't hesitate to open the fridge and ask me whether there is anything to eat in the house, although he knows there won't be.

It will be great to see him again . . . but in the meantime I'm sure going to miss him.

Chaos When 'The End' Arrives

We were not ready, but then how could we be ready for something like this?

It was something mankind had never experienced, so there was no way to prepare. Oh, there had been heated talk and stories on television, but no one takes those alarmist rumors seriously, do they?

It was the Christmas season, a time of peace for all mankind. That's what we thought, anyway.

I hung up the phone, the message I had received still sending shock waves through my mind. I had not been watching TV when the alert came, and it was my friend from across town giving me the news.

Rumors had been circulating wildly for days, but now, when we least expected it, the unthinkable was about to happen. If the news were true, and why shouldn't it be, I had only about 30 minutes to react. Only 30 minutes to prevent disaster. Thirty minutes until doom.

I tried to calm myself. No use rushing about without purpose, without a plan. My heart was racing, my mouth was dry. My head felt like it was going to explode from the pressure.

The store! I had to get to the store right now.

I rushed to the car and thanked my lucky stars I had remembered to buy gas. The word had spread across the city like wildfire. Everyone knew the time had come. Side streets dumped their traffic into the main routes like rain-swollen streams. Guys in four-wheel drive trucks were plowing up the median.

You could taste the fear in the air, a taste like sucking on a nail.

The shopping center parking lot loomed ahead. Cars were jammed into the lot in a crazy quilt pattern, as if a giant hand had reached down and mixed them up for the fun of it. Doors were bashed, fenders crumpled, bumpers twisted. But no one seemed to care.

People were rushing about pellmell like sharks in a feeding frenzy. There was no kindness, no civility, no Christmas spirit. It was every person for himself.

I finally stopped the car — I don't remember where or how — and joined the surging mob. I was filled with fear and rage, and I didn't hesitate to shove my way through.

I looked at my watch. Time was running out! It was coming, and I wasn't ready!

I thought the worst would be outside but what I saw when I shoved my way through the door will live with me forever.

People were hitting each other, snarling curses as they clawed for what they wanted, what they had to have, what they would die to get. It was a scene from Dante's Inferno, a town gone mad, a people destroying themselves from fear and panic.

I remember one little girl in a frilly dress with black patent leather shoes and matching bows in her hair. She couldn't have been more than 8, a lovely child. Her name was Mandy. Or Priscilla. Or Dawn. Something sweet like that.

She kicked the old grandmother in the stomach with one of those shiny Mary Janes and grabbed a package from the aging fingers. A young woman tried to stop her, and she bit her in a place best left unspecified.

Then there was the preacher. He was bravely trying to create order from chaos until the quiet nun with the guitar walked by. He bashed the guitar over her head and grabbed the package she was carrying. Foam flecks flew from his fat fingers as he wiped his fevered lips. He had his.

I saw a granny with a lovely granny smile and twinkling granny eyes and a homespun granny bonnet. She was wildly waving a machete as she cleared a path.

The clerks in the store had surrendered to the mob. One callow youth in a stock clerk's smock sat high on a shelf, cackling madly and snapping his fingers to the sound of Alvin and the Chipmunks.

Meanwhile, I was making my way forward, sometimes crawling, sometimes stepping over the carnage on the floor about me, sometimes walking right through it. Maybe I was lucky, maybe fate meant me to succeed, maybe the hand grenade helped.

These people were my neighbors, my chums, members of my church, guys I knew from the bowling alley, women from work. My boss' wife appeared in front of me. I got rid of her with one quick elbow to the neck.

Over in the TV department the news was the same. Hysterical announcers kept switching from city to city, repeating the now familiar scene.

I wondered what had happened. How had the civilization we had worked so hard to build and perfect gone bad so quickly?

What was there, in our hearts of darkness, to trigger this? What was there in our primal being that made us revert to animals at the slightest provocation?

We pretend, we dress in suits and follow the rules and then we go berserk.

It was then that I decided that it wasn't worth it. If it meant that I had to join the insanity about me, then to heck with it.

I don't know how I got out of the store. And I don't care. Maybe it was the grenade. But I made it out and slowly, with resignation, headed for home.

The end was coming. The final minutes were ticking away.

I felt a strange peace come over me as I made it home and sat down in my favorite chair. This is better, I thought, better that the end should come here, at home, rather than locked in a final struggle with desperate people.

I heard the car door slam and the excited sound of my daughter running toward the front door.

I took a deep breath and turned to face her, a forced smile on my face.

This would be the hardest part.

How would I explain to that smiling lass what was about to happen? How would I explain that Daddy, who could fix a bicycle, who could dry a tear, who could chase the boogeyman away, could not, on this Christmas, find a Cabbage Patch doll?

No Matter How Old, Daddy Is Daddy

This is what I got for Father's Day:

My daughter Denise came striding into the house yesterday with that wave of boundless enthusiasm, good humor and high energy that is her trademark. The screen door had not fully closed behind her before she bounced onto my bed and launched into a blow-by-blow description of her best friend's wedding the day before.

She had come to fix me breakfast. It was Father's Day and I was to be treated to breakfast in bed, an old family tradition on Mother's Day and Father's Day. I was looking forward to it. I have eaten perhaps a dozen and a half of those offspring-prepared meals, and while all of them were not of gourmet quality, they all had a healthy dollop of love in them that no haute cuisine could approach.

But I didn't get breakfast in bed this Father's Day. Instead I got a pleasant lesson in growing up for daddies.

We fathers of daughters are pretty nice folks, but we have one serious flaw: We refuse to recognize the fact that our daughters are going to grow up and become adults just as we did.

We tell them, in moments of huggy tenderness, that they will always be our little girls. They smile and think we are merely speaking philosophically, that we are expressing our love for them and making promises to always be there when we are needed. They and we daddies feel all warm and gushy inside when we say it — but they don't think we are dead serious.

Sorry, daughters, but we really believe it. You will always be our little girls. Like Peter Pan, you will never grow up. We'll be fixing bicycles and broken hearts for all eternity. You may get taller, but you'll always be a little girl.

And when we realize that we've been wrong — when we realize that although you will always be our daughters, you won't be our little girls — it can make us a little nervous,

I half-listened as she told me about the wedding — she had been the maid of honor or some such important duty in Donna's and Bill's nuptials — but my mind was a long way away.

This young woman perched on the end of my bed on a pretty Sunday morning in June was not my little girl — she was a 21-year-old woman. Her best friend had gotten married the day before and, in not very long, this woman has plans to follow her down the aisle.

I kept thinking, as she described how she caught the bride's bouquet (it would have taken a linebacker from the Dallas Cowboys to keep her from catching that symbolic bunch of flowers), that this wasn't some childish fantasy, some heart-stopping crush on a rock star. This was the real thing. My daughter is going to get married. Just like a woman.

It did not help when I thought of her younger sister. Melanie is 20, a junior at East Carolina University. When she calls me on the phone and we discuss what she's studying in college, she uses concepts and terms that make me try very hard not to let her know that I don't have any idea what she's talking about. I am experienced in giving meaningful advice on how to best understand the multiplication tables, but advanced sociology leaves me shaking my head.

Fathers are famous for knowing everyting, or being able to fake their little girl's socks off. But I realized sitting there in bed yesterday morning that my baby girl knows more than I do. Just like a woman.

One of my daughters is getting married, the other one is on the verge of becoming a social scientist, and I'm sitting there wishing they had a skinned knee that needed patching. I know how to do that. I can kiss it and make it better with the best of them. I'm good at hugs and sharing the comics on Sunday morning and teasing them about their latest boyfriends or that noise they call music.

I know how to be a father of two little girls, and if I do say so myself, I do it with a certain flair. I enjoy the job and I'm good at it and I don't want it to end. But it is going to.

I'm scared. I don't have any idea how to be the father of two grown women. I get along fine with grown women — but they're somebody else's little girls, somebody who is as befuddled as me.

They don't tell you about this part in Dr. Spock. There is a name for it when women suffer this rude awakening. They call it the empty nest syndrome — that time when the children have grown and flown and the mother is at loose ends with her life.

But what about us daddies? What do we do when a very nice young man, who is obviously goo-goo-eyed over your daughter and says he plans to marry her, merely holds her hand at your house and we want to yell, "Take your hands off my little girl, you cradle-robbing pervert!" Am I jealous of this very nice young man and that big college for taking my little girls away from me and teaching them they can live without me there to wisely tell them what to do and when, why, where and how to do it?

You bet I am.

They are grown and through being little girls. But I'm not through being a daddy — yet.

My Father's Day gifts this year were much more than a sweet card from my daughter off in college who is studying for summer school exams and a nice breakfast and entertaining conversation from my daughter who lives across town.

My gift this year was far better and more important. It was the realization that although our lives have changed, I still have a job as their father, and I'd better get on with learning how to do it.

It was a wonderful Father's Day present.